AF471183

She's Got What It Takes

DEANNA SIRLIN
She's Got What It Takes
American Women Artists in Dialogue

Jennifer Bartlett

Louise Fishman

Jane Freilicher

Joyce Kozloff

Elaine Reichek

Joan Snyder

Pat Steir

Ursula von Rydingsvard

Betty Woodman

CHARTA

Design
Fayçal Zaouali

Editorial Coordination
Filomena Moscatelli

Copyediting
Charles Gute

Copywriting and Press Office
Silvia Palombi

Promotion and Web
Elisa Legnani

Distribution
Anna Visaggi

Administration
Grazia De Giosa

Warehouse and Outlet
Roberto Curiale

Cover
Deanna Sirlin
Map, 2012 (detail)
Mixed media
10 x 5.5 inches
© Deanna Sirlin
Courtesy of the artist.

We apologize if, due to reasons wholly
beyond our control, some of the photo
sources have not been listed.

No part of this publication may be
reproduced, stored in a retrieval system
or transmitted in any form or by any means
without the prior permission in writing of
copyright holders and of
the publisher.

Edizioni Charta srl
Milano
via della Moscova, 27 - 20121
Tel. +39-026598098/026598200
Fax +39-026598577
e-mail: charta@chartaartbooks.it
www.chartaartbooks.it

For Phil
Because he's got what it takes

Contents

9   Acknowledgments

11   Where It Begins

17   Betty Woodman: Gesamtkunstwerk

27   Ursula von Rydingsvard: Power and Presence

37   Joyce Kozloff: Mapping the Life

47   Jane Freilicher: Always Summer

55   Jennifer Bartlett: Tending the Garden

65   Pat Steir: Art is Life

75   Joan Snyder: Getting It Right

83   Elaine Reichek: The Thread

93   Louise Fishman: Taking the Ball and Running

103   After

107   List of Illustrations

111   About the Author

Acknowledgments

I would like to thank:

Giuseppe Liverani and the entire staff at Edizioni Charta.

The artists—Jennifer Bartlett, Louise Fishman, Jane Freilicher, Joyce Kozloff, Elaine Reichek, Ursula von Rydingsvard, Joan Snyder, Pat Steir, and Betty Woodman—about whom I have written in this book. They gave me their time, honesty, and passion for art. Without the care of the artists' assistants and gallerists who helped me assemble photos and images, this book would not be what it is.

John Cheim and everyone at Cheim & Read Gallery for their gracious support of this book, their generosity, and their commitment to the women artists they represent as well as all the women artists whose work they admire.

Andrew Arnot, Eric Brown, and the staff of Tibor de Nagy Gallery for all their help.

The Parrish Art Museum for allowing me to use one of their archival photos.

Locks Gallery, Philadelphia, for finding archival photos of Jennifer Bartlett.

The board of *The Art Section*, who encouraged me to keep writing about women artists.

All the interns who have worked with *The Art Section*: Elise Dismer, Izzy Garcia, Hayley McIntyre, Arianna Mantas, Chelsea Aldrich, Sarah Betts, Kyle Pind, Marium Khan, and especially Evie Saleh and Maddy Booth. And of course Maria Haslett for lending me these wonderful young artists.

Susan Andre for kindly taking on the job of proofreader.

Kevin Salwen and Andrew Dietz for their help and support as writers.

Carolyn Budd and Steve McKenzie who helped me with my cover design, and Palmer Warner for her wonderful technical skills.

Hayden Herrera, my mentor under the Warhol Foundation/Creative Capital art writers mentoring program.

My beloved canines, who are my constant companions.

And of course Philip Auslander for teaching me to write beginning in 1980 and never giving up on this one long tutorial.

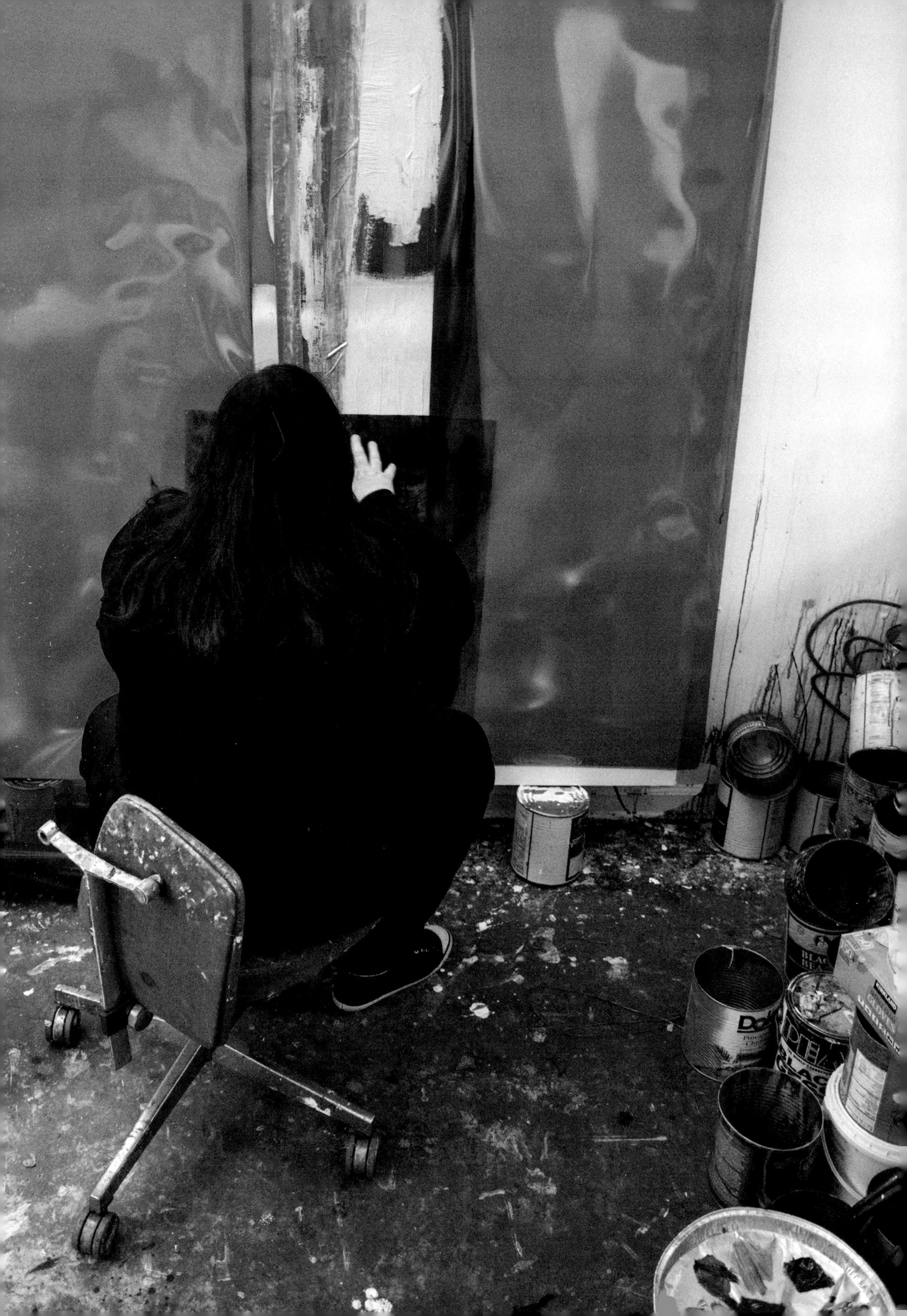

Where It Begins

I began this book when I first started writing articles for *The Art Section: An Online Journal of Art and Cultural Commentary*, which I founded in 2006 and of which I am the editor-in-chief. For the first time in my life as an artist who writes (yes, this is a category) I got to pick what I was going to write about. I had been writing a scant four to six art reviews per year for *Art Papers* since 1997, and I hardly ever got to pick the shows I reviewed. I worked under a myriad of editors, from the esteemed Glenn Harper, now at *Sculpture* magazine, who was a sensitive and insightful reader, to Sylvie Fortin, who spoke to me about the historical significance of one artist writing about another. She emphasized to me that it was not for the present that I was writing but for the future, and so that others could see these interrelationships. I had never before thought about my writing in this way, and she helped me to realize that the choice of subject was important and made a difference. At the same time, she made me feel I had less control than ever over what I was writing about. These sorts of limits were what challenged me to create *The Art Section*.

I knew I wanted to write about women artists, as I felt they were not being covered enough or in the ways I felt they should be. I was raised a feminist of sorts—my mother worked her entire adult life, and her passion was for her job—but my parents never really understood my being an artist. And frankly, with no women artists in the universities to serve as role models, and few in the museums, I am not sure I had the right tools either. I came of age at a peculiar time: post-Vietnam, post-civil rights, and post-women's movement. However, as a precocious child of the last baby boom, I was privy to what was going on in the 1960s and 1970s, if only as an observer. I witnessed change via the evening news on TV, and slowly in my schools and clothes and friends.

In high school I studied art with Suzanne Osterweil, who was young and beautiful; I remember her green eyeliner and red hair. In her classroom something different was at stake. My high school had race riots because of desegregation, but none of that behavior took place in her classroom. I think I learned a little about art but a lot about all kinds of other things there. Little did I know that I would never again have a female art teacher.

In college and graduate school, I never had a female studio art professor. Rosemarie Beck taught at Queens College of the City University of New York when I was earning my Master of Fine Arts degree there, but it was not until much later that I got to know her. It saddens me now that I did not get to study with her, but we did get to know each other quite well when she came to Ithaca, New York—where I was living at the time—to have an exhibition at Cornell University. We talked as artists about her paintings, her life, and her trials and triumphs.

I do not want to say I had no feminist art education or consciousness. I studied art history with Anne Sutherland Harris, who left mid-term to have her baby; she made sure we all knew about Judith Leyster and Rachel Ruysch, two Dutch painters of the Golden Age. And I read Hayden Herrera's biography of Frida Kahlo in my postgraduate stupor. I felt closer than ever to Kahlo's paintings from reading about her life, and although my experiences could not have been more different, I empathized with her as a woman artist.

When I met the artist Anne Truitt in the summer of 1983, we were both at Yaddo. I was there for an extended residency of nine weeks, something important so early in my career. Anne was extremely helpful and gave me some important mentoring just by revealing to me how she worked. Her strength and will were so evident in her work and person. When we met, I was a mere twenty-four and she was in her early sixties. Anne knew what to tell you—she told you what you needed, no more, no less. Her work has the same strength and clarity; it reveals to the viewer what the viewer needs to see and is able to see.

After meeting Anne at Yaddo, I saw her again one day in 1984 or so at the Phillips Collection in Washington, DC. Surprisingly, considering how different our work is, both of us were looking at the same cluster of

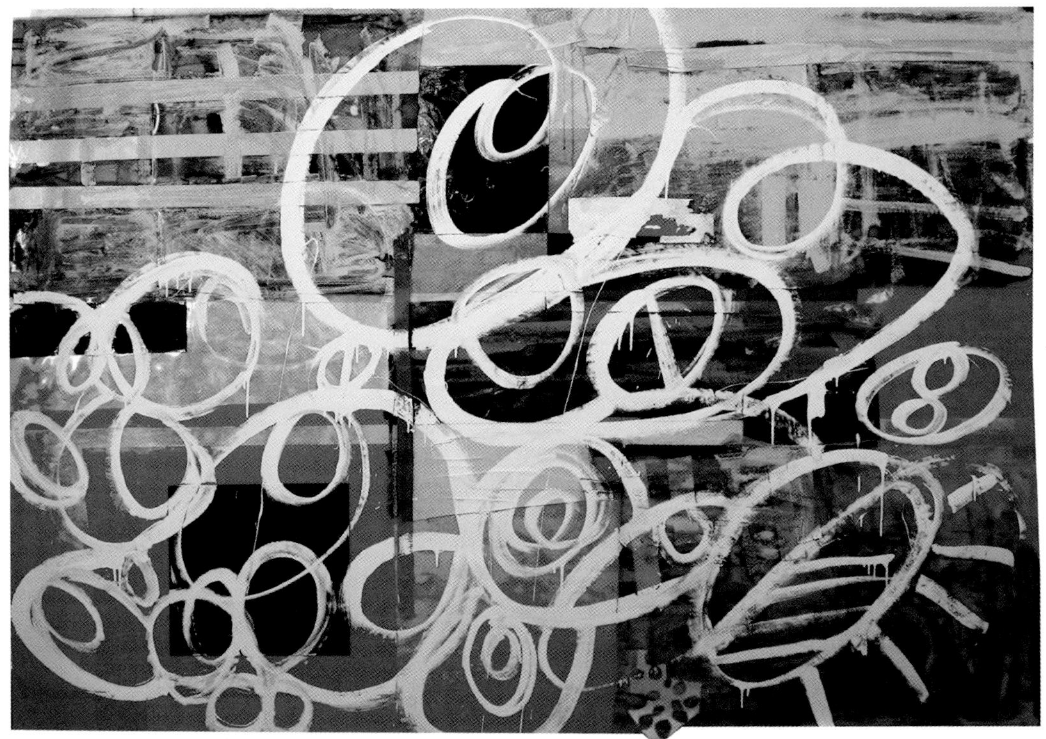

Bonnard paintings from the museum's permanent collection, which are almost always on view. I had recently read her published journal *Daybook*, which she wrote at Yaddo, and then her next book, *Turn*, also partially written there. I was living in Virginia at this time and made my way fairly often to DC. Delighted to see Anne, I revealed to her that I had recently read *Turn*. She asked what I thought about the book. I cautiously told her I found the book, which focused on working as an artist over a career that spanned thirty or more years by this time, a bit depressing. The book focused on the artist's passage through middle age and how it changes one in the studio as in life. I was still in my late twenties, and Anne was about sixty-five. She laughed and told me to read the book again in ten years and then tell her what I thought.

And indeed, a bit more than ten years passed before I picked up *Turn* again. This time I heard something different in the voice of the artist. Anne's voice rang triumphant rather than tired with effort and age. In my twenties, I still had many years to go before I would start to feel the physical difficulty of being an artist, the grind of standing all day or climbing up and down the ladder when working on large paintings, or being on one's knees when stretching canvases. Ten years later, I knew different and felt differently about the physical work that is often part of being an artist. In training my interns, who are mostly around seventeen or eighteen years old, I see that the physical tasks they are not used to are more difficult for them than for me . . . at least at first. In some ways, the years make it easier: the body has memory and knows without effort how to connect brush with canvas, and even stretching canvases is so much easier when your hands have been doing it for thirty years or more. But backs are more fragile, and bones break, making the physicality of being an artist increasingly difficult. So, when I reread *Turn*, I smiled. I was not at all depressed this time but understood from my own experience about the body and life of an artist and, of course, the importance of stamina.

In 2009 I traveled to Washington, DC, to see Anne Truitt's posthumous retrospective (she had died in 2004) at the Hirshhorn Museum and Sculpture Garden and to write about it for *The Art Section*. The exhibition moved me very much—the work was so like the artist in its beauty and directness. It was a luscious and compelling exhibition, arranged with such sensitive curatorial thought that I felt the presence of the artist. When looking at the works, I felt the brush in her hand painting layer upon layer of color onto the sculptures until they had a presence. I was sad that I could not send my writing to Anne, who right before her death was only just receiving the kind of critical analysis and respect that was her due.

This is when I thought about the women artists, like Anne, whose art I had looked at for thirty years or more. I thought perhaps I could talk to them about their art and gain a clearer understanding of both the person and the artwork. The longer I look at artwork, the more I realize that who the artist is, how she lives, works and, frankly, functions are all part of the process.

I chose the artists I discuss here on the basis of several simple criteria: they are all female, I have been looking at and drawing inspiration from their work for at least thirty years, and they are all still working. There are other artists like Adrian Piper, Lynda Benglis, and Jenny Holzer for whom the timing was not right but whom I hope to include in a future book. The essays assembled here are not works of art history or criticism: they are personal and reflect my appreciation of these women as a younger artist following them. The essays are based on visits I made with the artists, follow-up telephone interviews, and my own perception of their work and its meaning. There are, of course, male artists whose work I have been looking at for thirty years whom I could be visiting and whose work I could be writing about, but that is a different journey. By talking to the women who made these art objects I had been looking at, I hoped to learn more about their work and lives, and what has made it possible for each of them to be a significant artist making meaningful work.

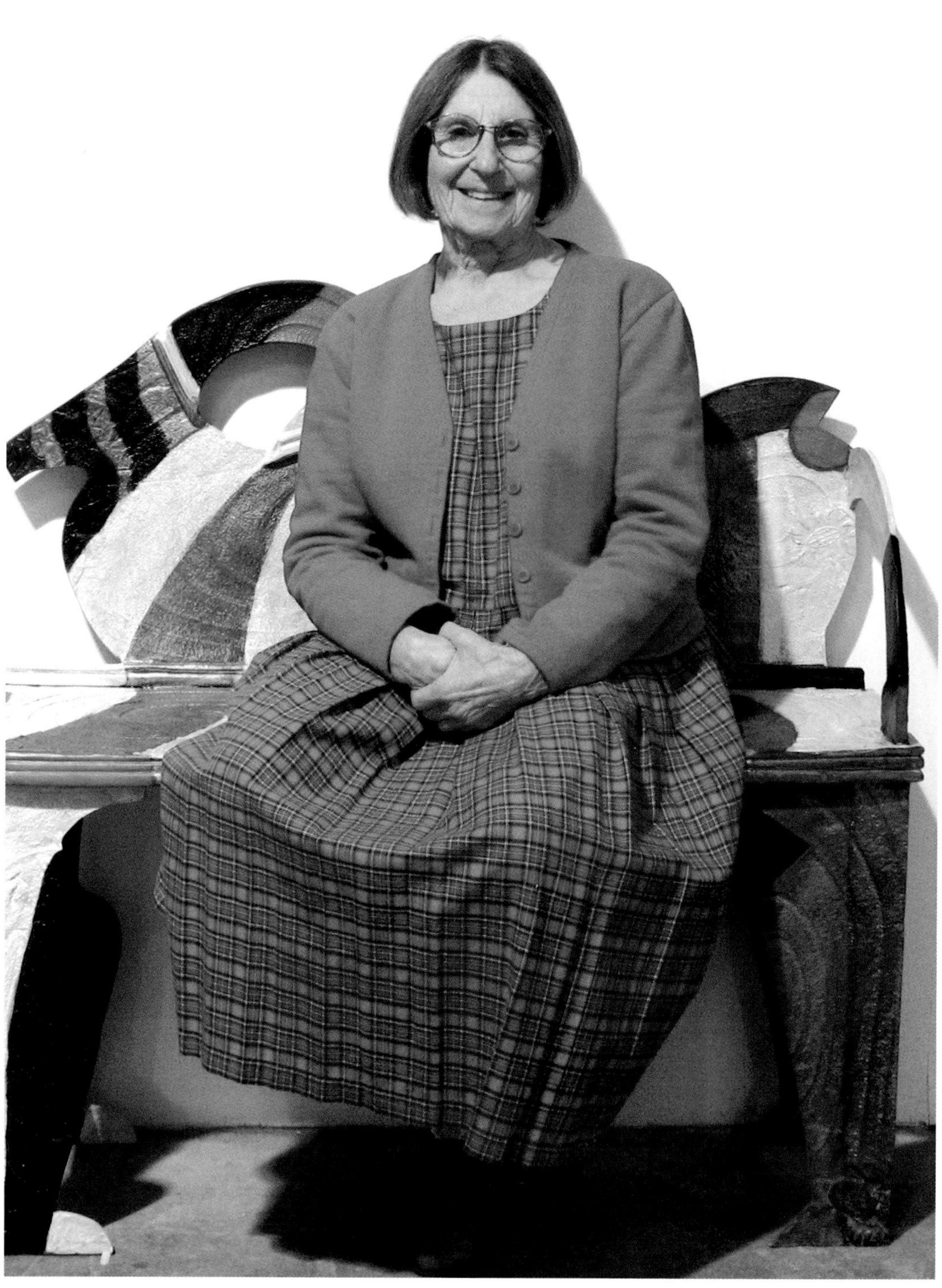

Betty Woodman
Gesamtkunstwerk

I

Rooms occupied by artists sometimes reveal their inner psyches, their work habits and preferences, as well the physical needs that must be met so that they can realize their ideas. Betty Woodman, who has been working with clay for over sixty years, divides her time between New York City and Antella, a small mountain town outside of Florence, Italy. For many years she also spent part of the year in Boulder, Colorado, where she and her artist husband, George Woodman, taught in the Art Department of the University of Colorado. She has shown all over the world, from the Metropolitan Museum in New York City to the US Embassy in Beijing and the Museo Delle Porcellane, Palazzo Pitti, Giardino di Boboli in Florence, Italy.

In the winter of 2012, Betty welcomed me to her NYC apartment and studio. I thought I had first met the Woodmans in Venice during the vernissage of the 2009 Biennale, but she reminded me that we actually met in Denver years earlier when I was having a show at a gallery where one of her graduate students was also showing in the next room. This makes me think that some cosmic rule of the art world is in play—that some artists' paths are meant to cross. I don't remember what we spoke about in Denver, but I do remember being struck by Betty's large eyeglasses and the keen gaze behind them that left nothing unobserved.

Betty's New York studio was warm and very bright to my eyes as I entered in late afternoon on a cold, gray, slushy January day. I sat on a bright pink plastic chair, while Betty sat on a delicately hued one. She did not look at me while we talked but always focused on her work. As she spoke about her life and work, I watched the light behind her go from that northern winter gray to a rich dark cobalt blue inside a window frame painted

Portrait of Betty
Woodman,
circa 2009

vivid yellow. This shift in light and color made all the works of art in the room look more intensely hued and seductive as we sat and talked.

On the studio walls surrounding us hung brightly colored drawings on paper. The tools of the potter—a wheel, tables, brushes, and glazes—were set around the room's periphery. Woodman's kiln was out of view, but I could faintly hear the white noise it produces. There were also new works being thought out, brightly colored canvas carpets of fuchsia and yellow or blue and black, and works in black and white with repeated linear patterns of three parallel lines lay on the floor. Large vases, bent and twisted, stood in the middle of the room and beckoned with a kind of sensual physical richness. Her studio is a complete world that encompasses the colors you sit on, the ones you look at flat on the wall, and the vases provocatively invading the space.

My compelling interest is in Betty's work and the continual inventiveness with form that has let her move beyond the wheel and into the painted world as well as the conceptual world of installation. Most ceramic artists have not pursued this kind of cross-pollination of ideas and formats. Although Betty tells me she is still quite tied to the ceramic world, she has been able to take great leaps in her oeuvre and is constantly refining and redefining her forms and herself. At eighty-three, she is still taking chances and making changes. She is not interested in resting on her considerable laurels, but in pushing ever forward to see how far she can possibly go.

From 1948 to 1950 Betty studied at the School for American Craftsmen—a school known for its ceramics department—while it was at Alfred University in New York State. She studied with Linn Phelan there, whom she cites as an important influence. He taught about ceramic form and how important it is to learn how to look. "Working was the most important thing; form and medium are what make ideas," Betty told me. After finishing her studies, Betty taught ceramics in numerous places in her hometown of Newton Centre, Massachusetts, and in the Boston and Cambridge area. She taught a course in ceramics in Cambridge where she met her future husband, the painter and photographer George Woodman, while in his freshman year at Harvard University. They have been married now for almost sixty years, and their artistic support of one another is part of the larger picture of their individual strengths. Betty describes George as

Betty Woodman
Peruvian Vase and Shadow, 1984
Glazed earthenware, epoxy resin,
lacquer, paint
23 x 28 x 15 inches
© Betty Woodman
Courtesy Salon 94, New York

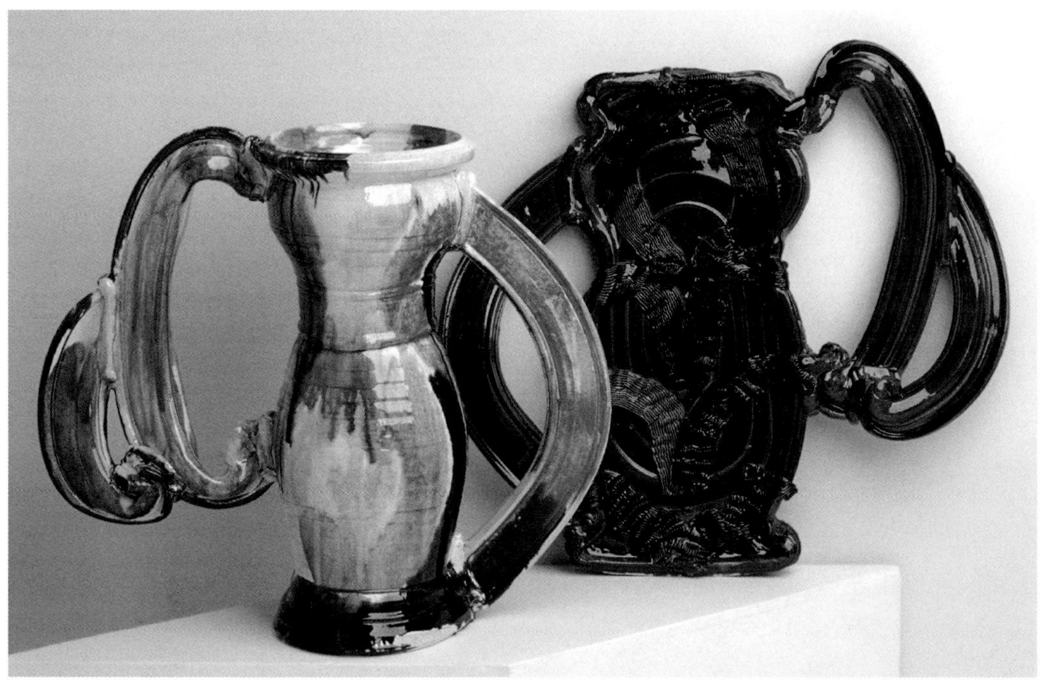

Betty Woodman
Installation view in the Cane Acres
Plantation House Dining Room
Playing House, Brooklyn Museum
February 24–August 26, 2012
Photo: Hiroki Kobayashi
© Betty Woodman
Courtesy Salon 94, New York

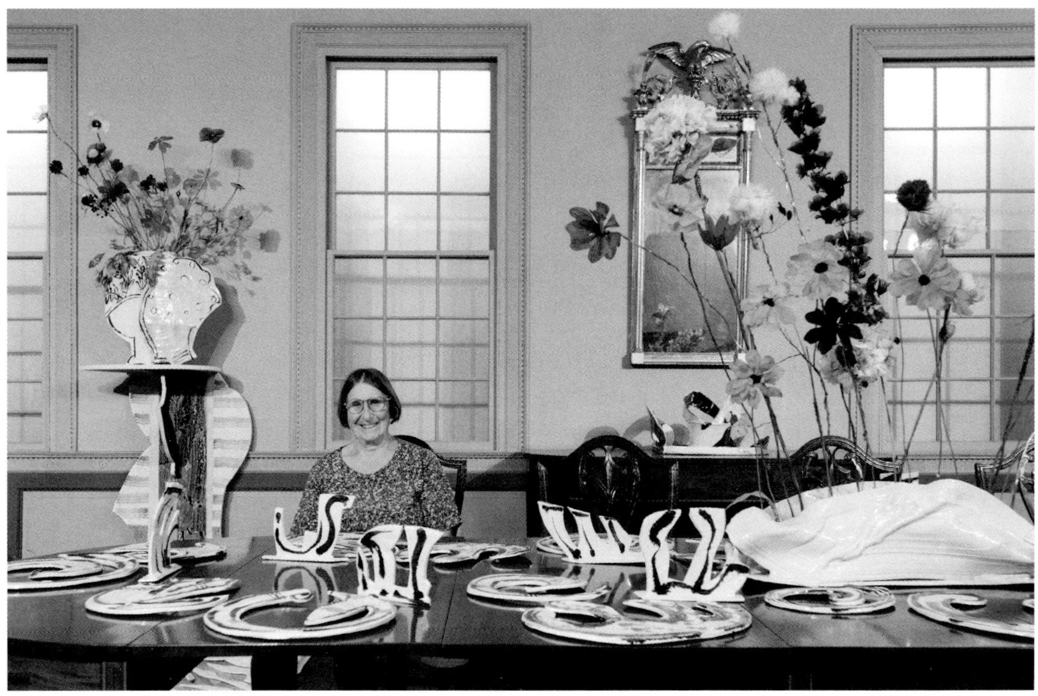

someone she can talk to about her work every day, and vice versa. She could not imagine anything less from her partner in art and life.

Betty came to ceramics as a production potter, which means she developed the skill and strength to make innumerable pots, plates, and mugs that are all similar in feeling and, of course, functional. This practice continues in ceramics classes. I know of schools where the student throws one hundred perfect tea bowls and at the end of the day destroys them all. This training is designed to instill the degree of confidence and control that makes one a master craftsperson, which the ceramicist who aspires to being an artist must also be.

During her years growing up outside of Boston, Betty spent many hours at the Boston Museum of Fine Arts. She told me about a Korean pot with a lid that she fell in love with and that made her want to be a potter. It is a small pot, regrettably not currently on view, though I long to see it; the first works that move one so much are important to see, to understand, and to feel. The Boston Museum has an amazing collection of great range and magnitude—just spending time with such objects was important to Betty's development. It trained her eye to understand form and, most importantly, she learned how to look.

Equally important to Betty were her trips to Italy. It was there she saw color used in what was to her a new way, especially in ceramics. Majolica, a low-fire pottery made in Italy, has a beautiful intensity of color and pattern. In 1968, after many sojourns in Italy beginning in 1951, the Woodman family, which now included son Charles and daughter Francesca, spent three months there and then found a house to buy in Tuscany. For many years the family divided their time between Italy and Boulder. In 1980, Betty and George bought a loft in New York to be more connected to what was happening in galleries there.

Although Betty began as a functional potter, a maker of small vases and pots that owed much to ancient pottery, hers were no ordinary vases: they were not only formally inventive, but she applied glazes the way a painter applies oil paint—the touch, the dip, the hue were all exquisite. Her work reflects her sensibility: at once playful and *in your face*. She is deeply invested in color relationships and the intensity of hue. Ultimately, it was these glazes and their interplay with the geometric shapes of the vases that

Betty Woodman
On the Way to Mexico, 2012
Glazed earthenware, epoxy resin, lacquer,
acrylic paint
34 x 35 x 9 inches
Photo: Eli Ping Weinberg
© Betty Woodman
Courtesy Salon 94, New York

drew me into the work. Over time, her work grew larger and became more painterly and sculptural. She continued making vases, but the handles became more architectural and wing-like: she threw them flat on the wheel, then cut them into geometric shapes before attaching them to the vases.

These wings are crucial to Betty's work. Because of their distinctive geometry, they function more as extensions of the vessel than handles with which to carry it. Betty takes generous liberties with glazing: the three-dimensional pot becomes a support for the spirited movement of color, which takes on a life of its own rather than functioning as decoration. By drawing additional vases on the surface of her ceramics, she creates a play between two- and three-dimensionality that recalls cubist space. In some cases, the glazing creates very different images with very different relationships to the shape of the vase on different sides, giving three-dimensional objects a defined front and back.

Betty also goes further by removing the wings from the vessels and attaching them to the walls behind them as untethered, free-form shapes. This approach is similar to artist Howard Hodgkin's abstract paintings, in which the painting exceeds the limits of the canvas and moves onto the frame and thus into the viewer's space. Her large painted walls are not autonomous paintings but environments against which the vases are seen. She thus transforms the ceramic vase from a sculptural object to a shallow relief to an installation in which she deals with the entire space of the gallery or room. She overlooks no detail in the presentation of her work: when she had her show at the Metropolitan Museum in New York (2006), Betty replaced the ever-present flower vases in the atrium with her own works.

Betty is a woman of power. She is physically strong from a lifetime of manipulating clay. Growing up during the Depression (she was born in 1930) must have made her want to make things that people could use. But her desire to make art rather than functional objects took over. She projects a strongly defined persona. Her outfit is youthful and funky; she wears big glasses made of small bits in multiple colors, knee socks and sneakers, and a patterned dress with a vest for warmth on top. Her outfit, like her work, is full of wit but rooted in functionality. Betty talked to me about what people wear: she told me that this year, the people she sees on the subway all have winter hats with a braid on each side, while artists continue to wear the all-

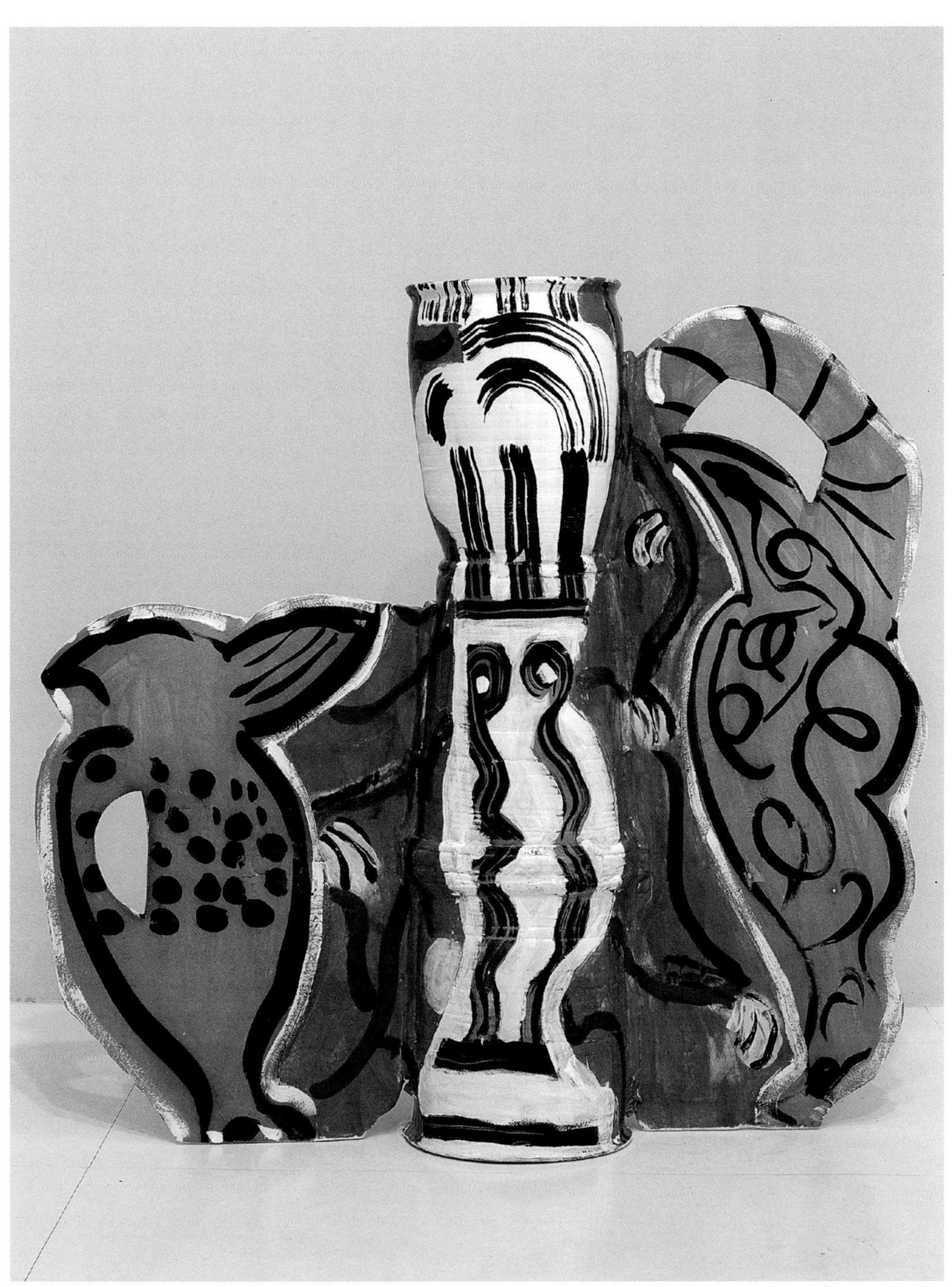

black uniform (I am guilty of this). She concludes that most people are fol- lowers, but she is not. It's true: she is not a follower but a player.

Betty tells me about a postwar building in a small town in Italy. The ar- chitecture was so impossibly ugly that the mayor convinced her to design a new façade to be painted on the side of the building to disguise it. I love the way this project participates in the tradition of painted buildings in Italy, with their wonderful ochre and green stuccos. But this painting creates the illusion of giant red cubist vases on a wall. An architectural mess is now reinvented as an art object by Betty's intervention. The building so im- pressed the mayor of the town where the Woodmans live in Tuscany that he asked her to paint a building there as well, but this hasn't happened.

Portrait of Betty Woodman, circa 1996 Photo: George Woodman

II

It is winter again, just at the end of the year 2012. Betty was the first of the artists I reconnected with by phone to bring everything up to date. There was a delightful ease in our conversation that was not as present when I visited her studio. Women of my generation and hers both know how to use the phone, and we were able to talk freely about her life and work. We discussed her upcoming shows, changes in the direction of her work, and her desires for it. Betty explains that she is an artist just because that is who she is: an artist.

Betty was asked by Barry Harwood, Curator of Decorative Arts at the Brooklyn Museum, to propose and curate an exhibition for the museum's period rooms in the spring of 2012, which she entitled "Playing House." The antique objects set in the period rooms reconstructed within the mu- seum meld with contemporary artworks that are a kind of intervention into these interiors. I remember these rooms quite well from my years of wan- dering through the Brooklyn Museum, where I took art classes as a child. These rooms were almost always empty of visitors and dimly lit in a way that was kind of dramatic but, in the eyes of a child artist, lacked some- thing. Betty asked artists Anne Chu, Ann Agee, and Mary Lucier to join her in this artistic action. There is a wonderful photo, similar to the one re-

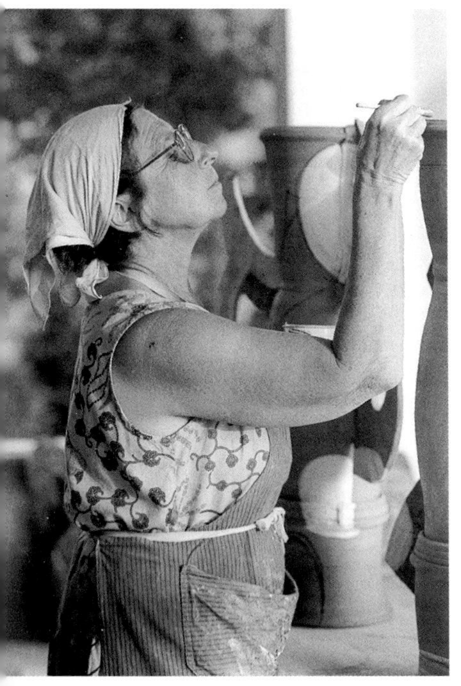

produced here, of Betty in one of these period rooms setting the table with her work. On the floor are her painted canvas and ceramic rug sculptures, and there are Woodman vases around the room in which Anne Chu placed her fabric flowers. The show was so successful that I believe such interventions will become recurring events.

Betty is about to have several gallery shows in Europe. I asked why, finally, there was this interest in her work. Betty said it was the art world, not she, who suddenly found clay to be an acceptable medium. As she put it, we are at a moment when the world of art, craft, and design "goes with me."

Other things have changed as well. Betty's work is less like pottery and more like large-scale, low-relief painting and installation. It is not, she tells me, that she feels differently about ceramic forms, it is just that her emphasis has shifted to painting and sculpture; ultimately, she is interested in combining all three. I feel her work has become a Gesamtkunstwerk, a term Wagner coined to describe his conception of opera as a total, all-encompassing work of art. I can almost hear Betty smile over the telephone. Yes, she would like to do sets and costumes for an opera, and Handel would be best because she loves his music. All that's needed is for someone to ask her to do it.

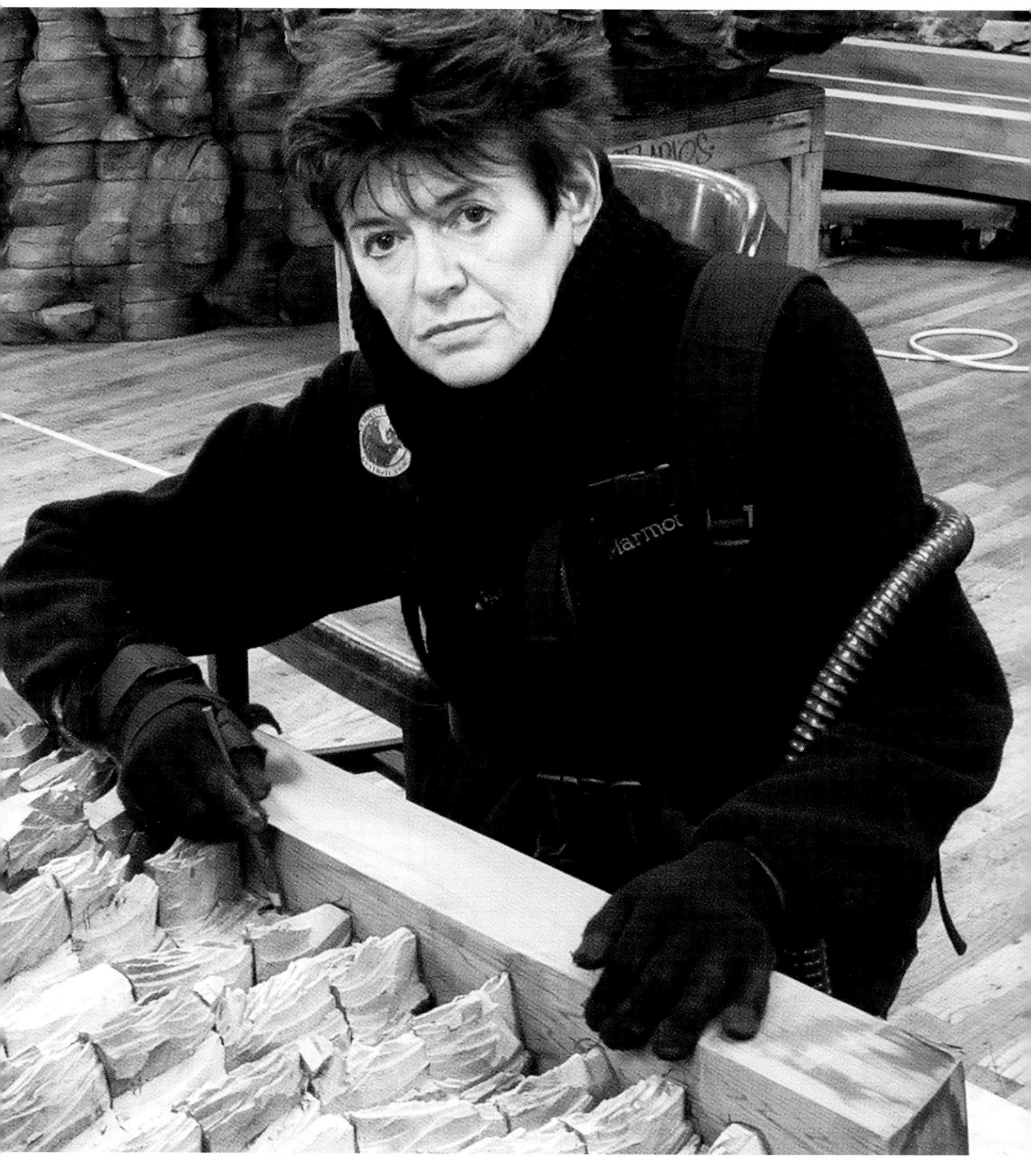

Ursula Von Rydingsvard
Power and Presence

I

There are some works of art that, when you first encounter them, fill you with the kind of emotion that can knock you over. When I first saw ancient Greek Kore and Kouros figures, standing upright with such power and presence, a surge filled my body in an intensely physical reaction. When I first climbed the stairs at the Louvre and saw the *Winged Victory of Samothrace*, I experienced an equally strong emotional charge. The first time I saw Ursula von Rydingsvard's sculptures, I felt the same way: I felt the work in my body before I really saw it with my eyes.

I first saw Ursula's work when I was living in Queens, New York, in the late 1970s. An artist friend told me about an artist whose work they thought would interest me. I am sorry to say I do not remember whose suggestion this was, but I followed it and went to see Ursula's exhibition at 55 Mercer, a cooperative gallery in Soho.

At the time, of course, there was no searching the web to see if I was really interested in this artist's work, so I went to the exhibition with no advance knowledge. I remember walking upstairs to the gallery, which was kind of dark. When I reached the top of the stairs and saw Ursula's work, I felt immediately as though the air had been sucked out of my lungs, so primal was the impact. This artist used wood in a way I had not seen before. Until this moment, all of the contemporary sculpture I had seen was made of metal, stainless steel, plastic, acrylic, bronze, stone, or marble. Whereas these are cold mediums, I felt that in Ursula's work the material and the artist were locked in a warm and loving dance; the sculptor's sympathetic relationship to her medium was palpable. Although there are many other sculptors whose work reflects harmony with their mediums, there was something different here, something more. There

Portrait of Ursula von Rydingsvard with *Conjugation*, 2012
Photo: Andria Morales
© Ursula von Rydingsvard
Courtesy Galerie Lelong, New York

was an immediacy for which the parallel in painting is *alla prima* or direct painting.

When I met Ursula, she said she did not recognize the term *alla prima* but confirmed that she works directly in wood with no models, drawings, or studies: just planks of cedar, the graphite of her pencil, and the power tools she uses to carve the wood. She also revealed her admiration for Alberto Giacometti, the twentieth-century Swiss artist. She envisions her cedar planks as pieces of paper. Giacometti built his sculptures by looking at one vantage point, one piece or mark (in a drawing) at a time—from that the overall form grew. In Ursula's practice, the work grows and takes shape by her working directly with each plank, rather than using a study or mockup.

In 2011, I received an e-mailed press release from SculptureCenter in Long Island City, New York, which is just across the bridge from Manhattan, announcing Ursula's show there. I decided to call Ursula, who was delighted to meet with me. We made plans to meet first at the gallery and then travel to her studio in Brooklyn.

Right before setting out on this journey I went to the High Museum of Art in Atlanta to see the Vogel Collection, a series of works, mostly on paper, from the 1970s. On view were two of Ursula's lovely medium-sized drawings (always the most difficult size). The drawings are of light articulated with lines that get more or less dense as the light falls across the space. The High Museum also owns a sculptural work of Ursula's. *Five-Fingered Comb* (1994), made of cedar and graphite, hangs on the wall. Purchased for the High Museum's collection by Susan Krane, who was the curator of Modern and Contemporary Art at the time, it is a wonderful relief sculpture of medium scale that elegantly evokes both a comb and fingers.

I made my way to SculptureCenter, arriving before the artist in order to have some time alone with the work. I was immediately struck by the cast resin work in the courtyard that marked the entrance to the exhibition. *Elegantka* (2011) has a translucent bluish hue, and at ninety-eight inches it towered over the crowd. A group of college students from Oregon was visiting the exhibition, and an older student boldly and loudly announced that she had no need for anything else they had seen in NYC: this show was it!

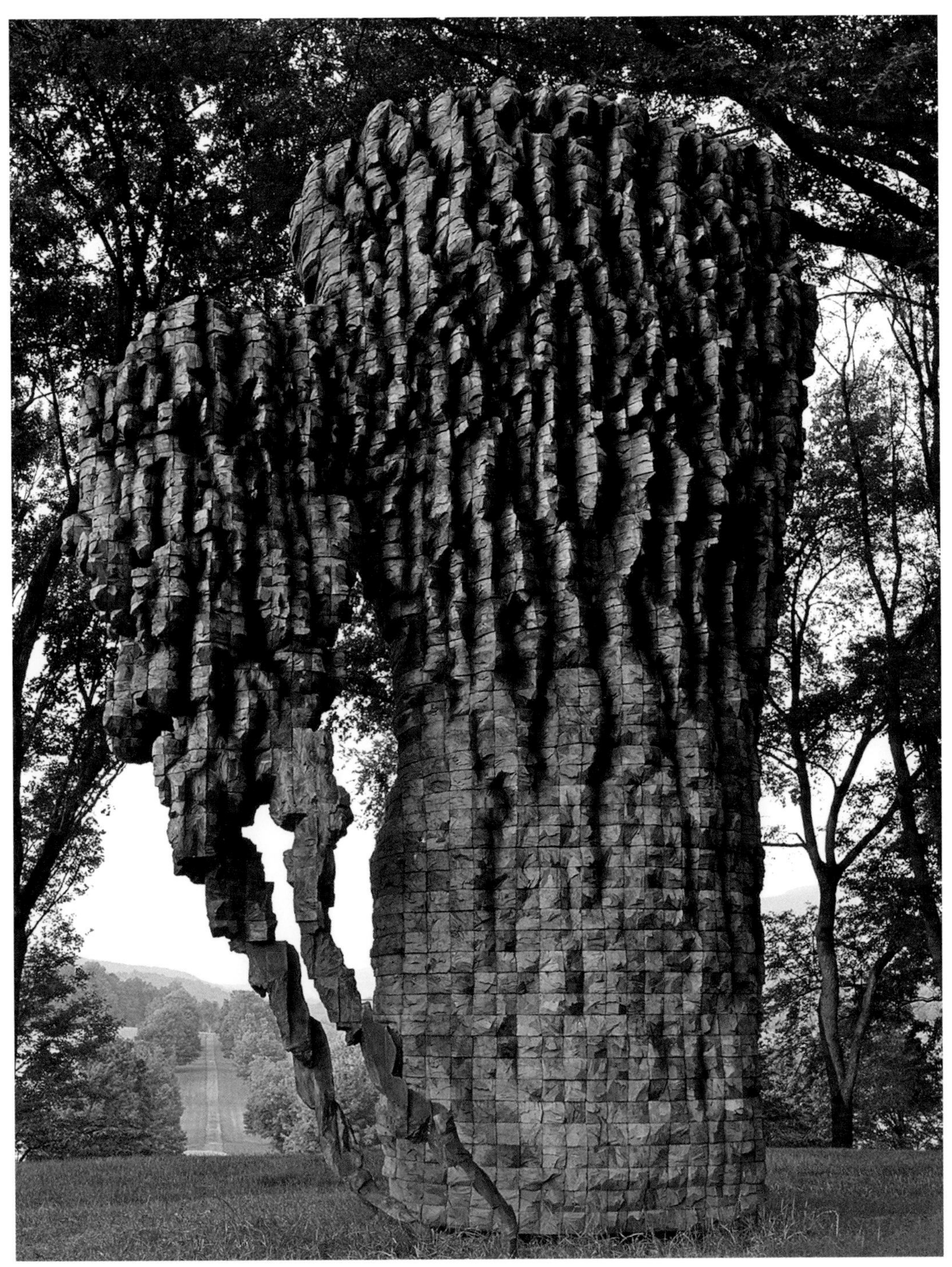

Ursula arrived and quickly realized that I was the traveler meeting her. I told her about the students; they smiled rapturously as she spoke with them. And it was a show that demanded rapture. The works were placed with an eye to creating a dialogue with each other and the viewer. I stood close up and ran my eyes over the multitude of carved marks made with either a saw or a graphite pencil. As I moved back, I stayed in the works; their forms opened to me, revealing their scale and volume.

The works speak to one another. *Wall Pocket* (2004), made of cedar and graphite, is over twelve feet tall and stands upright in the gallery like an ancient tree trunk of which all that is left is the crevassed base, large enough for a person to stand inside. It is made of cedar planks that von Rydingsvard draws on and cuts with a saw so that the facets read as if Mother Nature had made them—though this Mother Nature has power tools! The process is complicated: the selection of the cedar trees, the cutting of the planks, the gluing of the layers, the drawing and notations on the wood, the artist's reading of these notations like musical notes to be played with her tools. *Krasavica II* (1998–2001), six feet tall and twenty-two feet long, stands along the wall like a row of the proud, beautiful women to which the work's title refers in Russian or Ukrainian.

In the center of the space is another large work, *Droga* from 2009. Fashioned from cedar and graphite, it lies in the center of the gallery like the fallen torso of a great tree or some large animal stretched out into the space. *Droga* is the feminine form of "dear one" in Polish, and this is how Ursula means to title her sculpture. But "droga" means "drug" in many languages (including Czech, Italian, Polish, German, Spanish, and Swedish), and it also refers to intoxication or spice. *Droga* is an intoxicating work; the twists, turns, and mass of this great form made me want to lie beside it and absorb all I could from its presence.

On the right side of the gallery entrance were five massive wall pieces, *Five Lace Medallions* (2001–2007), each just under ten feet high and four feet wide in cedar, graphite, and chalk. Each is a rectangle containing a strong horseshoe shape and a structure below it. Ursula shows them side-by-side, filling the gallery wall with a powerful structural presence.

Arriving at the studio from SculptureCenter, Ursula tells me what I as an artist do not want to hear: "This does not get any easier!" Her downstairs studio is massive, filled with works in all states of completion, many lovely even though unfinished. Upstairs is a large drawing studio, a light and airy place populated with paper pieces being thought over and created. Ursula introduces her assistants; they understand who Ursula is as an artist so clearly that they can perform for her as parts of herself, like the Hindu goddess Kali's multiple arms.

There have not been many woman sculptors that are able to make work on the scale that Ursula has achieved. I ask her about who has been helpful to her and mentored her as a sculptor. Ursula sites as influences women artists like Louise Bourgeois, her long-term studio mate Judy Pfaff, and her friend Kiki Smith. These three women are all sculptors, and their friendship must have been important when there were so few woman working in the medium. I ask Ursula if she ever had a woman teacher in college or graduate school, and she says there was one named Jean Linder who taught sculpture at Columbia University graduate school.

I comment on the beautiful light outside the studio, and she says proudly that this is a part of New York City where the buildings are low so you can see the sky. Ursula draws great inspiration from the city. She is an observer of this great microcosm: the diverse multitude of people all setting out to do their jobs and live their lives, its ebbs and flows from morning to night. I also see the weavings and pots she has collected over the years, but she does not speak of them; perhaps she knows that I can see the connection between them and her work, and that is enough. We talk of being an artist, how hard it is yet how necessary it is to go on. Since meeting Ursula, I have been reflecting on this person who not only makes work of the highest caliber but also runs a studio with multiple assistants. Her assistants have all been with her for some time; they do not speak while they are working, but do a dance of movements and gestures they nevertheless understand. They eat together, they work together, they make art possible together. Only Ursula actually makes the art, but her assistants help bring her ideas into being.

What are the qualities that make a person able to do this thing, to make art? For Ursula, I think it is an intense kind of sympathy that can be heard in her voice, a unique voice that expresses great certainty but also great empathy for the world around her. I want to describe this rhythm but I am unsure how to explain the intonation, the sympathy and empathy, in which you can hear the compassion that is, I think, where she finds the quiet place within herself to make her work.

Ursula was born in Germany, one of seven children, to a Polish family during World War II, obviously a traumatic time. After the war ended in 1945, she and her family lived in refugee camps for displaced Polish people in Germany from the time she was three years old until she was eight. Her family then moved to Plainville, Connecticut. You can tell Ursula has spoken of her background many times, and that it is not her favorite way of talking about what she does or how she came to be who she is. Her parents were hardworking, uneducated but not unintelligent immigrants whose primary goal was survival through hard work. Ursula, too, works very hard to create her art. Although Ursula's past—having had so little as a child, and having had to take inspiration from the barest of circumstances—does not provide a full explanation of how she has come to make this work. Yet her experiences have surely helped her to develop both the strength and the empathy that she uses to create her art—and that are reflected in it.

A young friend who read about Ursula in *The Art Section* knew Ursula's elder sister, a distinguished math teacher in one of the tougher public high schools in the Atlanta area, recently retired at the age of seventy-seven. When I mentioned this to Ursula, I could feel her smile over the phone. Right before she retired, two of her students misbehaved and received detention as punishment. In this case, detention meant they would have to keep up with her as she fast-walked around the school's track. They ended up trailing behind her. It must have been quite a sight: two seventeen-year-old boys unable to keep up with a lady in her seventies. I think Ursula and her sister may share the energy and determination to take on the world and live fully through every moment and situation.

II

It is the end of the day, it is winter, not that cold but extremely gray, and I phone Ursula to be brought up to date on her work. Her assistant answers

Ursula von Rydingsvard
Damski Czepek, 2006
Polyurethane resin
132 x 406 x 364 inches
Photo: Etienne Frossard
© Ursula von Rydingsvard
Courtesy Galerie Lelong, New York

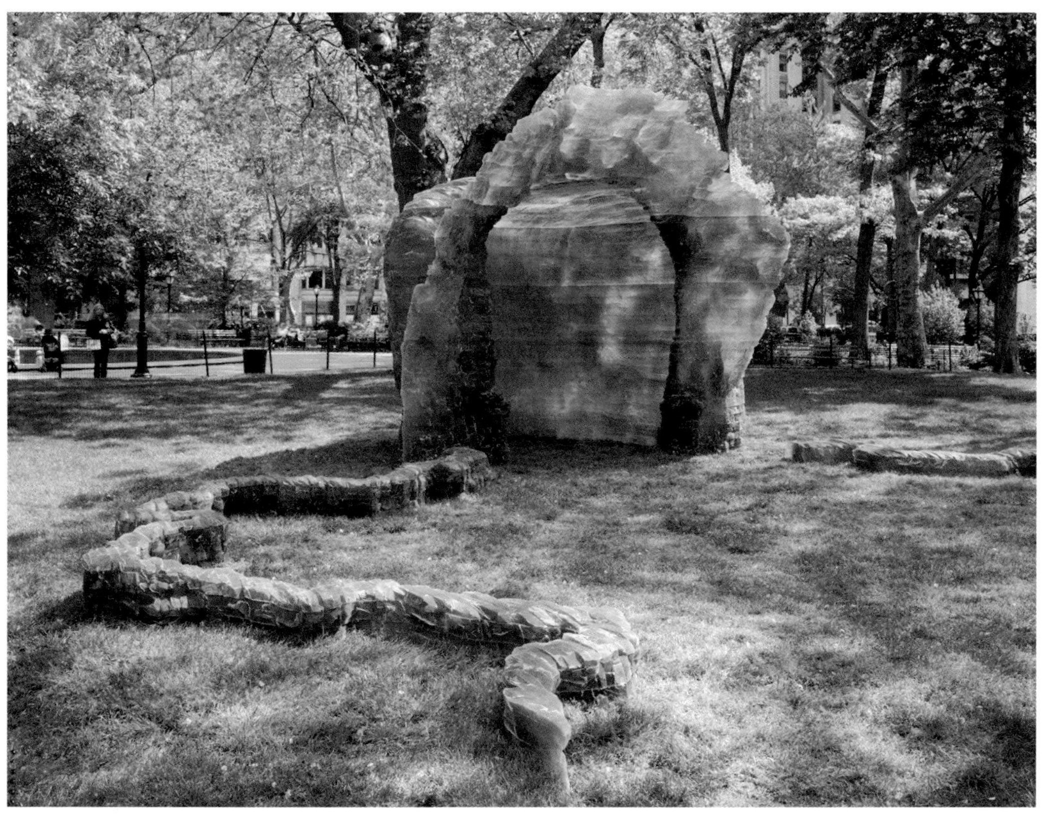

the phone, puts me briefly on hold, and then I hear Ursula's lovely cadence. There is something in her voice that is so soothing—I am glad to speak with her. She is curious about what I might need from her, she says, since really nothing has changed since we last met. But that is not true at all, for Ursula is continually working toward clearly defined goals. She tells me about three new projects, each one larger than the last. I am delighted to hear this, as I think her work should be in places where people can see it, be with it, meditate on it, and find it familiar, like a tree you always looked at or played on as a child. And when you return it should be there in its rightful place. I cannot believe she has taken on so much, yet it is just what every artist wants: to make significant work for places where it will be seen and appreciated.

Ursula has been asked for a piece to be located at the front of the East Wing of the National Gallery of Art in Washington, DC.

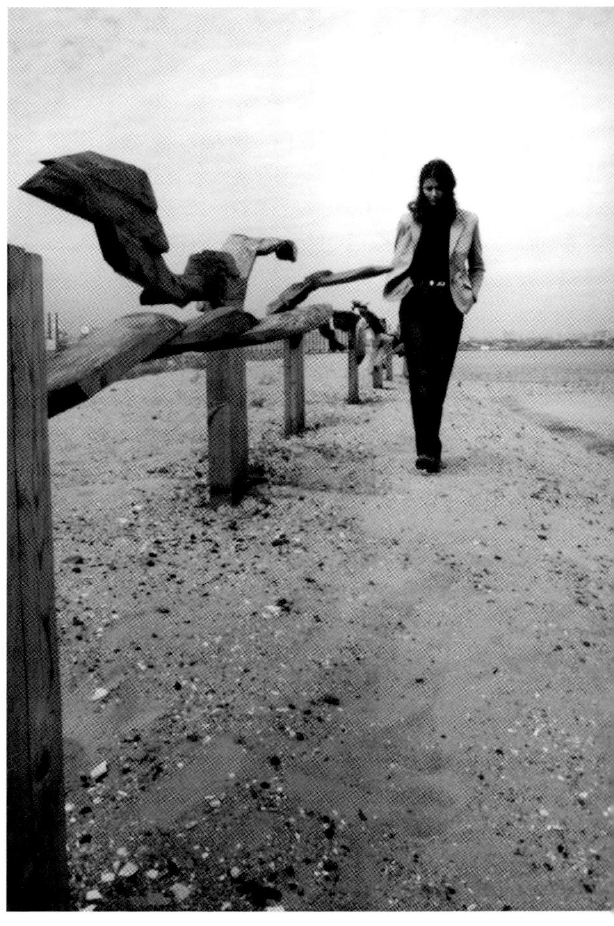

Ursula von Rydingsvard at Battery Park City landfill, New York, with *St. Martin's Dream*, 1980
Photo: David Allison
© Ursula von Rydingsvard
Courtesy Galerie Lelong, New York

When I was last there to visit the museums and galleries, the artist Roxy Paine was installing one of his pieces. There is a delicious irony in having a work by Roxy next to a work by Ursula. Both address nature; in fact, both simulate trees in particular, but the works are completely different in sensibility. Paine makes his trompe l'oeil trees out of stainless steel, each shiny metal limb a lifelike portrait of a specific branch. Ursula's work is organic in medium and form, but it does not mimic nature the way Roxy's does. She works with natural materials to recreate the grandeur and solemnity of nature on her own terms.

Ursula will be having a one-person exhibition at Yorkshire Sculpture Park in England. She already has two works in the park. When she was there recently, she found the site of her dreams. It is an old quarry that has not been mined since 1924. It is in a vast horseshoe shape that might become, under her gentle hand, a kind of sanctuary for reflection and meditation. The work is fully composed in her mind. She not only has the ability to realize such work, but also has the need and drive for such a large undertaking. She describes to me in detail how she will go about constructing the work, what materials she will use, how it will look, and what it will take to realize a project of this scale and scope. We agree that it only takes money, since her concept and vision are already so completely in place.

In a way, this project would reaffirm Ursula's relationship to earthworks and land art, already evident in some of her earlier work. In the early 1980s, Ursula and other young artists used the barren land in what is now Battery Park on the southwest side of Manhattan. *St. Martin's Dream* (1980) consists of a flock of winged forms deployed in a line across a sand dune. In an early work, *Song of a Saint (St. Eulalia)* from 1979, a large group of tall, thin cedar rods stand stoically on a hillside. About three-quarters of the way down, each pole has a botanical-seeming bulge, like a seedpod. During the winter, when the landscape is desolate, they suggest the promise of rebirth, while during the spring, when surrounded by lush green grass, they refer to fecundity. For *Tunnels on the Levee* (1983), Ursula carved out small interior spaces from the landscape using square cedar logs. Her structures seem like bridges from above and caves or shelters from below. On the phone, Ursula revealed to me her love for Giotto. Giotto's frescoes for the Arena Chapel (1305) constitute an installation that fills the space with an emotive power that Ursula also seeks with her cedar sculptures. Whether in interior or exterior spaces, her forms surround and envelope one in comfort and grace.

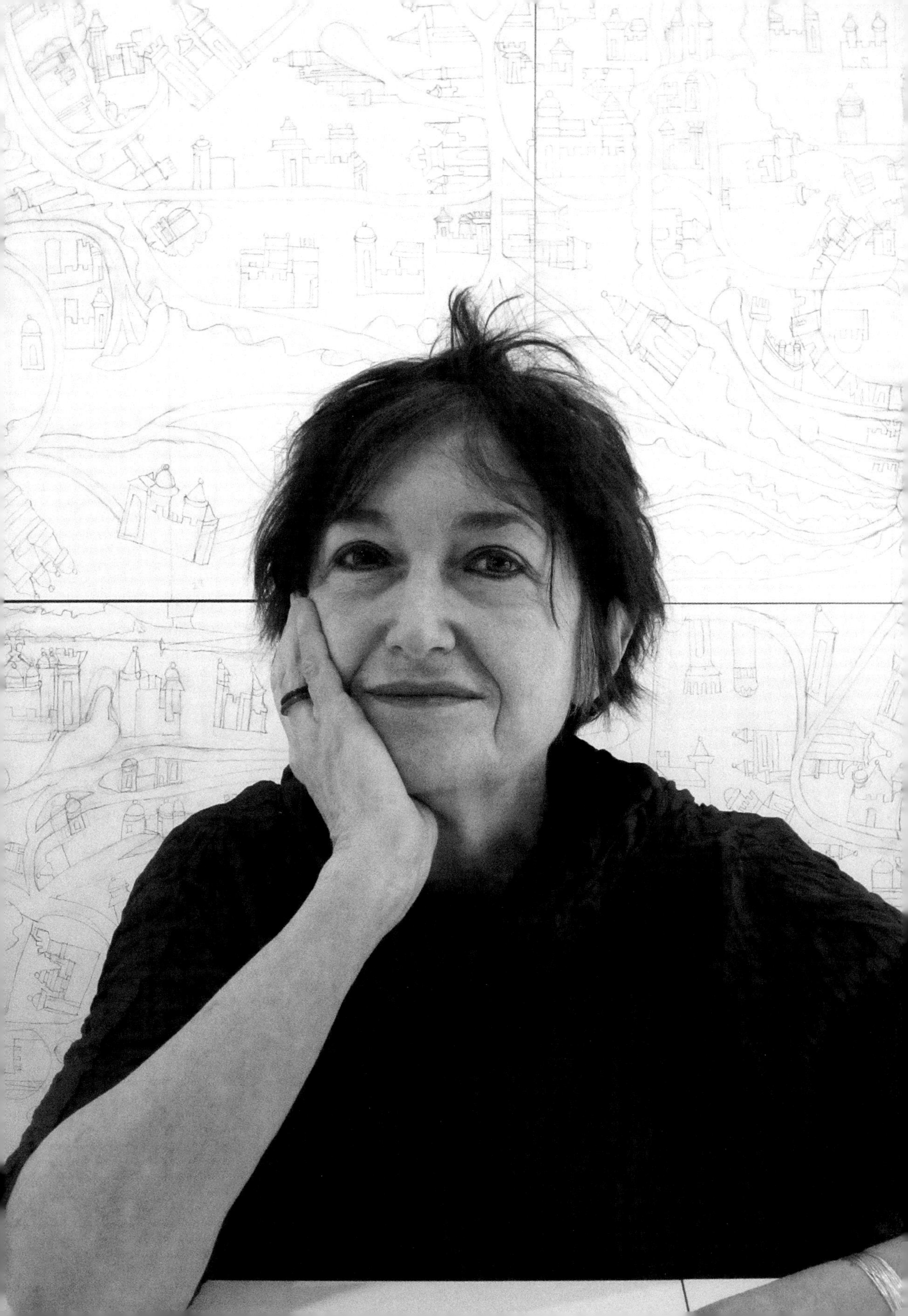

Joyce Kozloff
Mapping the Life

I

I do not know how, but I got lost in Soho while looking for Joyce Kozloff's studio, even though I had walked these streets since the 1970s while on my way to galleries or maybe a performance of The Wooster Group. Here I was, going to visit an artist who has devoted her work of the past twenty years to mapping the universe, and I couldn't find her place! My frustration was dispelled immediately, however, by the warm welcome extended by Joyce and her husband Max upon my arrival. Max, the distinguished artist and critic, served as barista, making us a fantastic espresso that we enjoyed with mysteriously salty yet delicious croissants. I felt at home with these people, as if I had known them from the New York neighborhood where I grew up. When the coffee was finished, Max left us to do his own work and we moved into Joyce's very large studio, which was just a few feet from the kitchen. She was working on *JEEZ* (2011), a twelve-by-twelve-foot circular map painting. Joyce was making the work in multiple square panels that hung in a grid-like fashion on the wall as she painted them; the large work was split in half down the middle so that each half could be reached without a ladder.

Joyce played an important part in the beginnings of the feminist art movement, and she was one of the key figures in the Pattern and Decoration movement of the 1970s. Joyce is a political person; she speaks about the past with such passion and immediacy that one might think it was just last month that she joined the women's movement and helped foster the feminist art movement in both California and New York City. But that is not why I am interested in her work. What I find compelling in Joyce's work first of all is the seduction of color and form that derives from her engagement with maps, targets, globes, and many art forms from cultures around the world. She has a natural affinity for color and uses highly saturated color in much of her work.

Joyce Kozloff in front of *JEEZ*, 2011 (in progress)
Photo: Morgan Rachel Levy

Her earliest works are abstract and come out of the Minimalists' use of the grid. In a large, sixty-by-sixty-inch painting from 1970, *To Vuillard (Red and Green)*, the canvas is divided into twelve rectangular parts; some shapes in the top half of the painting mirror counterparts in the bottom half. An audacious blue horizontal rectangle spans the midsection of the painting and serves as a border between the halves. All the rectangles have subtle divisions; some are divided by straight lines, others by pointy triangular forms similar to those found on a backgammon board. Joyce's paint handling is delectable; she uses acrylic paint in washes that emulate watercolor and are laid one on top of another so that the touch of the artist's hand is visible. The colors are diverse. The red and green mentioned in the title are present, of course, but so are ochres, Prussian blues, cerulean blues, and verdant greens that have been iced up. The painting evokes the intensity of a Vuillard, whose French interiors of the last century featured claustrophobic flowered wallpapers and sunken figures that blend into their patterns.

With *Three Facades* (1973), also in acrylic on canvas and handsomely tall at seventy-eight by sixty inches, Joyce jumps into the world of Pattern and Decoration. This painting contains three different patterns inspired by the tile and brick facades of Churrigueresque churches that she saw near Puebla, Mexico. There is a certain softness to the way the paint has been applied that makes the painting seem almost like a carpet or tablecloth hung out to dry, and the underlying grid evokes decorative patterns found in functional objects such as tiles and fabrics. The center panel is the most vibrant, with star-like shapes that sit inside diamonds. Each star shape and the color behind it is different, and each one is pleasing to the eye. They are very much like Josef Albers's paintings in his *Homage to the Square* series, though Joyce's compositions do not resemble Albers's simple arrangement of squares that he repeated over and over again. The similarity lies, rather, in the way the changing relationships of color shift and pulse in the viewer's eye.

For twenty years, from 1983 until 2003, Joyce was not primarily a studio artist but concentrated instead on large-scale, permanent public art installations. These works incorporate glazed tile and mosaic, with floors made from marble cut by Italian artisans. They are magnificent works: compositions of color and line that speak significantly of place, whether in the form of hand-painted maps of all the cities on the 44th parallel, or glass and ce-

Joyce Kozloff
L'Afrique, 2012
Acrylic, collage, and archival inkjet print
35.75 x 31.25 inches
Photo: Kevin Noble
© Joyce Kozloff
Courtesy DC Moore Gallery, New York

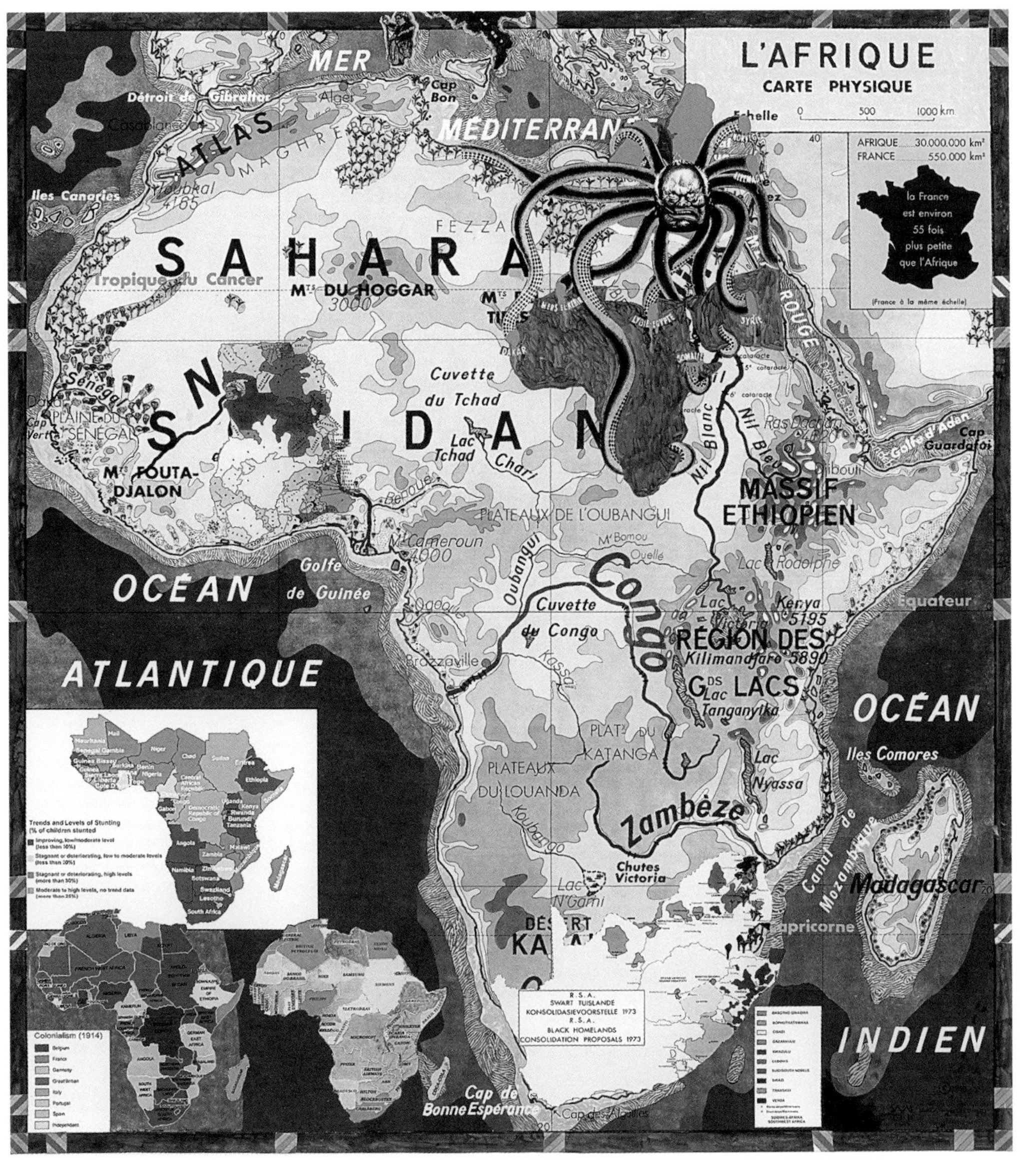

ramic tile works for a Philadelphia suburban train station that evoke the visual culture of the railroad in a bygone era. As a public artist myself, I know from personal experience how engrossing and demanding such commissions are. Handling the multiple demands of community, architecture, and government is never simple. Joyce is not sorry she pursued this kind of work, but you can tell when she speaks of her public art installations that she remembers both how wonderful and how exhausting it was to paint the tiles.

Although Joyce's overall compositions and the shapes of the tiles she uses evoke the traditional patterns she has studied in the harems and baths of Turkey and Morocco, her use of lighter and thinner color is entirely personal. Joyce broke with the traditional palette of highly saturated and solid ultramarine blues, verdant greens, and alizarin crimsons, replacing them with oranges, pinks, and soft warm greens. In many of the early works, Joyce repeats patterns and forms but changes the color, surprising me repeatedly with her choices. Where I least expect it, a lime green pops up next to warm red purple. The tile work is exquisite, but Joyce's physical and individual touch with the underglazes makes clear that it is the work of an artist who wants to bring a fresh, painterly approach to a traditional medium, rather than that of a craftsperson who seeks to simply continue a tradition. Given the chance, Kozloff's work will take over a space. She has covered walls and floors and hearths and bathrooms and any thing or place that can be covered with her work. She creates complete environments—an ambition I admire.

There is, of course, something obsessive in an artist's desire to fill a space with her imagery. But this obsessive quality and Joyce's attention to the articulation of form, and especially color, are among the many things that distinguish her art from decoration, even in the work she refers to as "decorative art." The tiles around her *Cincinnati Fireplace* (1980) are in only two shapes, a star and a hexagon, which are repeated in the same pattern row after row. Examined closely, however, each tile proves to be a world apart from its neighbors either by virtue of contrasting color or because of images she painted onto them. The repetition of the tiles and pattern is almost hypnotic, but the variations cause us to look at individual tiles as well as the over-all effect; we begin to perceive shapes made up of clusters of tiles that transgress their linear arrangement. Joyce's 1984 Wilmington Train Station entrance is based on a similar interplay of repetition and difference, this time creating an immersive environment in three dimensions. At first, the tiles on the walls seem to be arranged in horizontal bands distinguished by the size and shape of the tiles and by palette. Looking more closely, however, one starts to see variations within the bands that give individual tiles identities that syncopate the overall rhythms. When my eye moves around these fabulous spaces decorated with patterns appropriated from Frank Furness's architecture, I feel transported to a kind of postmodern version of Topkapi Palace: there are new palettes and a different sense of rhythm here, but the place has been imbued with similar opulence.

Like Tiffany or the Arts and Crafts movement, the Pattern and Decoration movement challenged traditional distinctions between art, craft, and design. In keeping with this approach, in 1981 Joyce made a series of artworks on which she collaborated with other artists. She and Betty Woodman made several functional ceramic works that were distinctly Kozloff in their use of Islamic star patterns. The cups and saucers Betty threw for Joyce were flatter than Betty's usual rounded forms, giving Joyce places to work.

Like her work in tile, *JEEZ*, the giant painting Joyce was working on in her studio, involves cultural appropriation. It is based on the Ebstorf Map, a circular medieval map of the world from thirteenth-century Germany that is twelve feet across and painted on thirty goatskins sewn together. Joyce has made her work the same size as the original. At the top of the original map is the head of Christ. Joyce is reworking this image, including rivers and oceans, which she paints in a luminous light ultramarine blue. In the original, a circular image of the world is inscribed in a square and surrounded by columns of text describing the creation of the world. Joyce is replacing the text with multiple images of Jesus drawn from a vast array of art-historical sources. There are baby Jesuses and adult Jesuses; thin Jesuses and fat Jesuses; black Jesuses and white Jesuses; medieval, Renaissance, African, and European Jesuses; there is even a Jesus that looks like the famous red poster of Che Guevara. There are a total of 125 Jesuses in the painting.

In the upper-left-hand corner are two iterations of the "Baby Jeez," as Joyce humorously likes to call him. He is nude in both images, but he is presented very differently. The one on the far left has his eyes open as a spigot of milk streams past him like some supernatural laser beam of nature's bounty. His body is thin and angular. The second Baby Jeez is asleep, plump, and softly bathed in a painterly glow. The face of another Jesus, standing above him, is painted like a totemic mask. Joyce's cross-cultural articulation of the "Jeez" is both a serious mediation on religious belief and a playful cross-cultural representation. As she says, "One usually sees just one at a time. It's funny to see so many, like seeing a bunch of Santa Clauses on a street corner."

My visit is nearing its end, and I decide to use the restroom before leaving Joyce's studio. I open the door and witness, on the walls of her bathroom, the most exquisite tile work left over from other commissions. It is inlaid floor to ceiling with colors ranging from red to orange to blues and purples, with floral drawing overlaid on a geometric pattern of borders within borders. No harem bathroom could be more beautiful than this one that the artist has made for herself and her family. Here, Kozloff remixes her own work the way she has long mixed and juxtaposed artistic styles from multiple cultures and centuries. It is as if her cross-cultural explorations and love of maps brought her home to this most personal space, which she has transformed into a private world of seductive color. It is a wonder.

II

Speaking with Joyce on the phone reminds me that she is someone who questions and instigates, a delight for me to listen to as she describes bodies of work like *China is Near* (2010), a series she made about Chinatown after her trip to Mainland China was cancelled, or the poster she made in which she renamed all the streets in Manhattan after women.

After learning she would not be visiting China after all, Joyce walked a few blocks from her home and found herself in the midst of New York's Chinatown. For the first time in her career as an artist she found herself photographing a visually overloaded urban landscape filled with knock-offs, color, signage, and an abundance of stuff. Joyce presents these prints as double-page spreads. A photograph of Chinatown kitsch appears on

Joyce Kozloff
Cincinnati Fireplace, 1980
Glazed tiles, board
60 x 114.5 inches
Photo: Ron Forth
© Joyce Kozloff
Courtesy DC Moore Gallery, New York

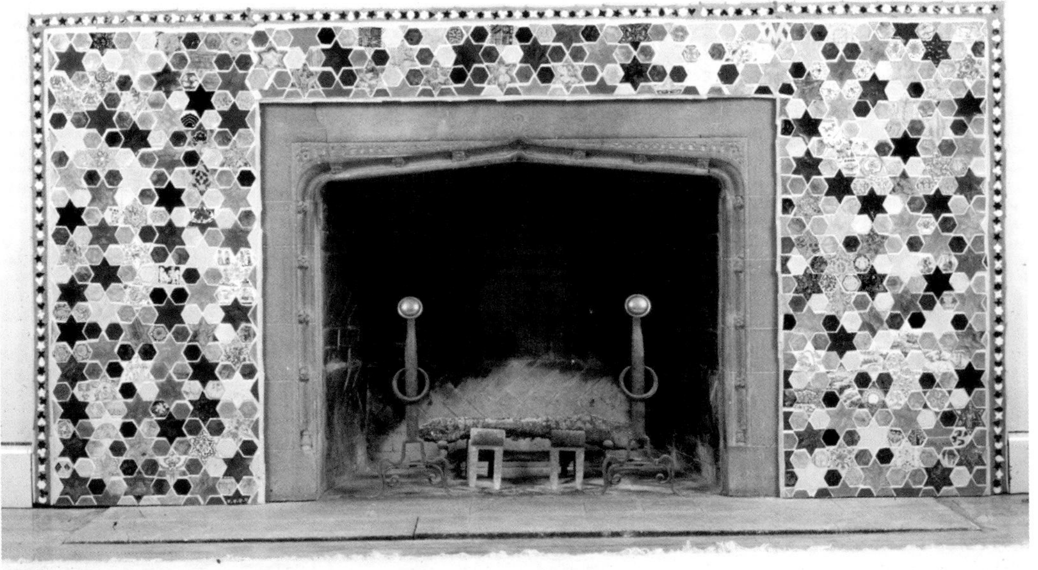

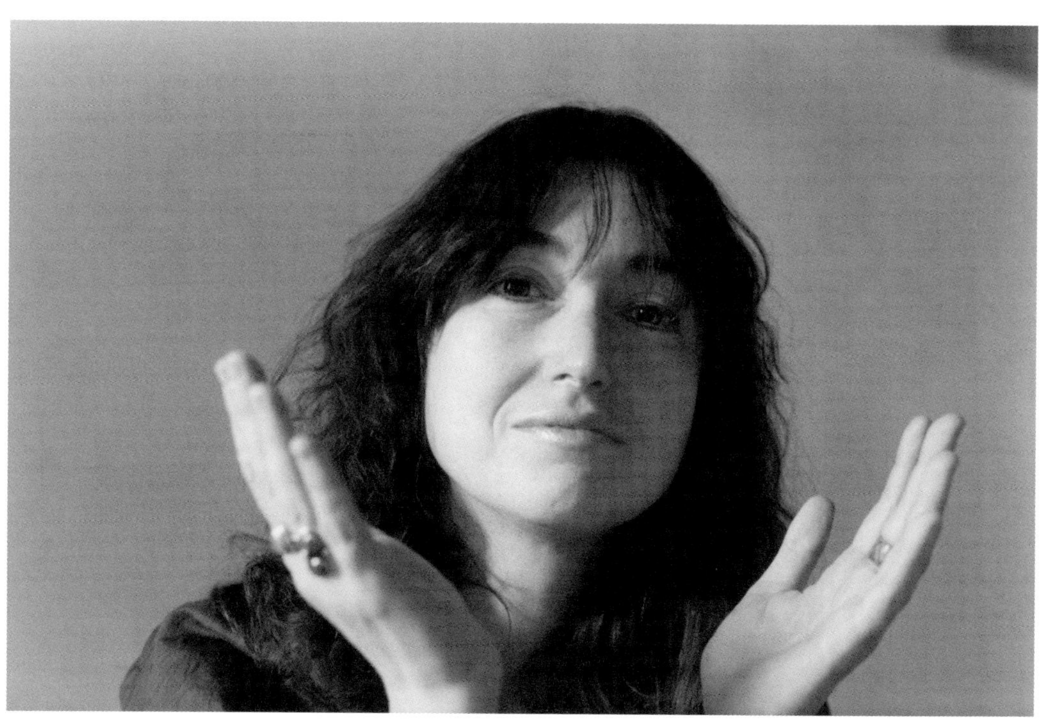

one side, juxtaposed with a print featuring Joyce's trademark maps and cultural borrowings. *See No Evil* is a particularly lovely page: at the bottom left, on the photographic side, are small statues of monkeys covering their eyes, ears, and mouths; moving upward on the same side, we see herds of miniature elephants strung together in colors of white, a deep dark red, and turquoise green. The other side of the fold is one of Joyce's maps of China with a wonderful decorative marking that depicts water. Sitting just in the center of the map is a large, painted golden chrysanthemum backed by the same turquoisey green of the elephants. Completing this mise-en-scène is a small black and white panda with bamboo in the bottom right. The left-hand side of the collage is a found image of repetitive forms, while the right-hand side, in mixed media, offers a symbolic image, since the chrysanthemum has many meanings in the Far East, mostly related to lamentation or grief. These prints, split down their middles, read as a visual book that Joyce created after making the prints.

Joyce has become a visual junkie, perhaps by nature or perhaps because the world we live in is so saturated with imagery. Every morning she reads *The New York Times* from cover to cover to stay informed. She is addicted to researching her imagery on the Internet. Type in a destination and you can see almost anything or anyone you want information about. In her most recent series of digital prints, *Social Studies* (2012), Joyce worked from a group of maps used in French schools in the 1950s, which she found in a flea market in Paris. Working at the Digital Arts Studio at Carnegie Mellon University through a residency, she integrated into these maps the most incriminating information she could find in her Internet research about the continents and countries pictured. Back in the studio, she continued to cut and collage and revise these to teach a wholly different lesson in Social Studies. Joyce has made a luscious overlay of pictorial commentary on the way these places were, are, and how they might change. The works themselves are a cornucopia of formal riches, with lush saturated color laid flat over the countries depicted in the maps. The maps become very surreal in Joyce's hand; a large squid or octopus at the top of some images extends its tentacles threateningly into the world. Men in tomato-red uniforms wear pointed hats and carry large guns. Even at Joyce's most surrealist moments, she is at the same time still acutely political.

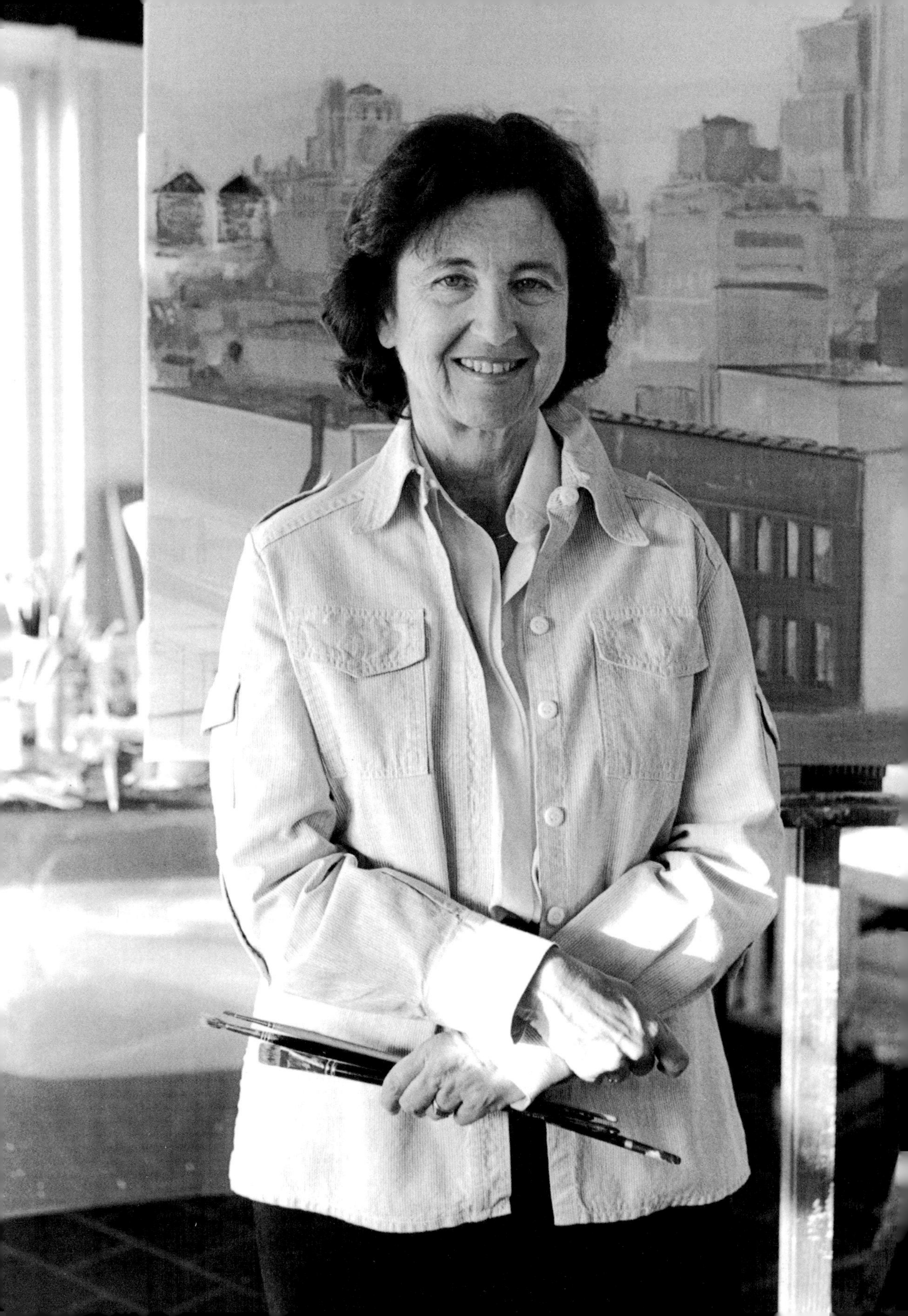

Jane Freilicher
Always Summer

I remember having in my college dorm room a calendar featuring the work of women artists. The calendar was big, with nice color plates. Jane Freilicher was one of the twelve painters in this calendar. I remember her image well: a squarish composition with a lusciously hued blue sky painted in a flattened manner, and a table mostly obscured by a vase of flowers centered on it. I also remember the calendar's having a painting by Mary Cassatt and I am sure something by O'Keeffe. I loved that calendar and wish I had kept it.

It was also the year I started to notice things like the fact that I had no female studio art professors. There was a woman photographer coming the next year who was described as someone's famous daughter. I do not remember her, but I do remember her work, which was photos of bread baking.

Many of the artists I talked with in the course of researching this book asked me, "Whom else are you visiting?" I happily give them the list. These are artists I treasure; they have been with me a long time as my friends in the studio, although I have never met them. When I mentioned Jane Freilicher to the other women artists, they smiled, nodded, and said, "Yes, Jane." I ask if they know her, since an introduction makes it all so much easier, but they all shake their heads no. Nevertheless, she is important to all of us, an American woman artist who has been painting for more than sixty years. A potted plant or vase of flowers on a table or shelf with the New York cityscape behind it, or a landscape seen from her studio window out on Long Island in the Hamptons have been her continuous motifs over six decades of painting.

When I meet Jane Freilicher in 2012 she is eighty-seven years old. She has agreed to meet me at her gallery, Tibor de Nagy, which has represented her since 1954, rather than her studio. Her studio is in her home,

Jane Freilicher,
1984
Photo: Nancy
Crampton

and her husband is not well (he subsequently passed away). I hope to get to the gallery early to see her show and her work before I meet her, but she is already waiting for me at the front desk, half an hour early. We go to the back of the gallery where there is an intimate space with her paintings, beautifully hung. Jane begins to talk to me about her work. She is extremely modest. She talks of her night painting that was so recently on her easel at home but is now hung in the gallery. She seems delighted to see her work there; she says it's sort of amazing that people seem to want to look at her paintings, and that they like her work. Jane comes across as a very private person; her talk with me is very modest, but leavened with a kind of humor that I have not run into for a while.

I recently listened to a radio broadcast of Jane, with her dear friend the poet and art critic John Ashbery, in which her wit was quite evident. They behaved like an old married couple spewing one-liners at each other, a game or habit that brings a bit of levity to the art of remembering things past.

Tibor de Nagy Gallery was quite a place "back in the day," as they say. New York School poets like John Ashbery, Kenneth Koch, James Schuyler, and Frank O'Hara all hung around the gallery, and some collaborated with visual artists on prints and text. They were all great admirers of Jane's work. I look at photos of Jane taken by John Gruen, a writer, who was married to the painter Jane Wilson (she also showed with the gallery). They were part of a charmed group in the Hamptons in the 1950s: Jane appears in many shots with Willem de Kooning and Lee Krasner as well as Frank O'Hara. Jane was glamorous; Gruen even took a photo of her entitled *Jane Freilicher (in film star pose) Water Mill, NY, 1958.* You can tell they were all having the most wonderful time.

At the Tibor de Nagy Gallery, she also met the painter and critic Fairfield Porter, with whom she developed a close friendship. Together they painted the bucolic world of eastern Long Island, a fresh, clear place where artists could work. Porter and Freilicher both used the landscape—with family members and friends naturally milling about, reading, painting, and sleeping—as a motif in their paintings. In 1954, Porter painted a double portrait of his wife, Anne, reading and Jane painting in the lush Long Island landscape. Neither sitter is paying him much attention, but the figures sit well in the composition. Another of Porter's Long Island pastorals

Jane Freilicher
Study in Blue and Gray, 2011
Oil on linen
24 x 24 inches
Photo: Alan Wiener
© Jane Freilicher
Courtesy Tibor de Nagy Gallery, New York

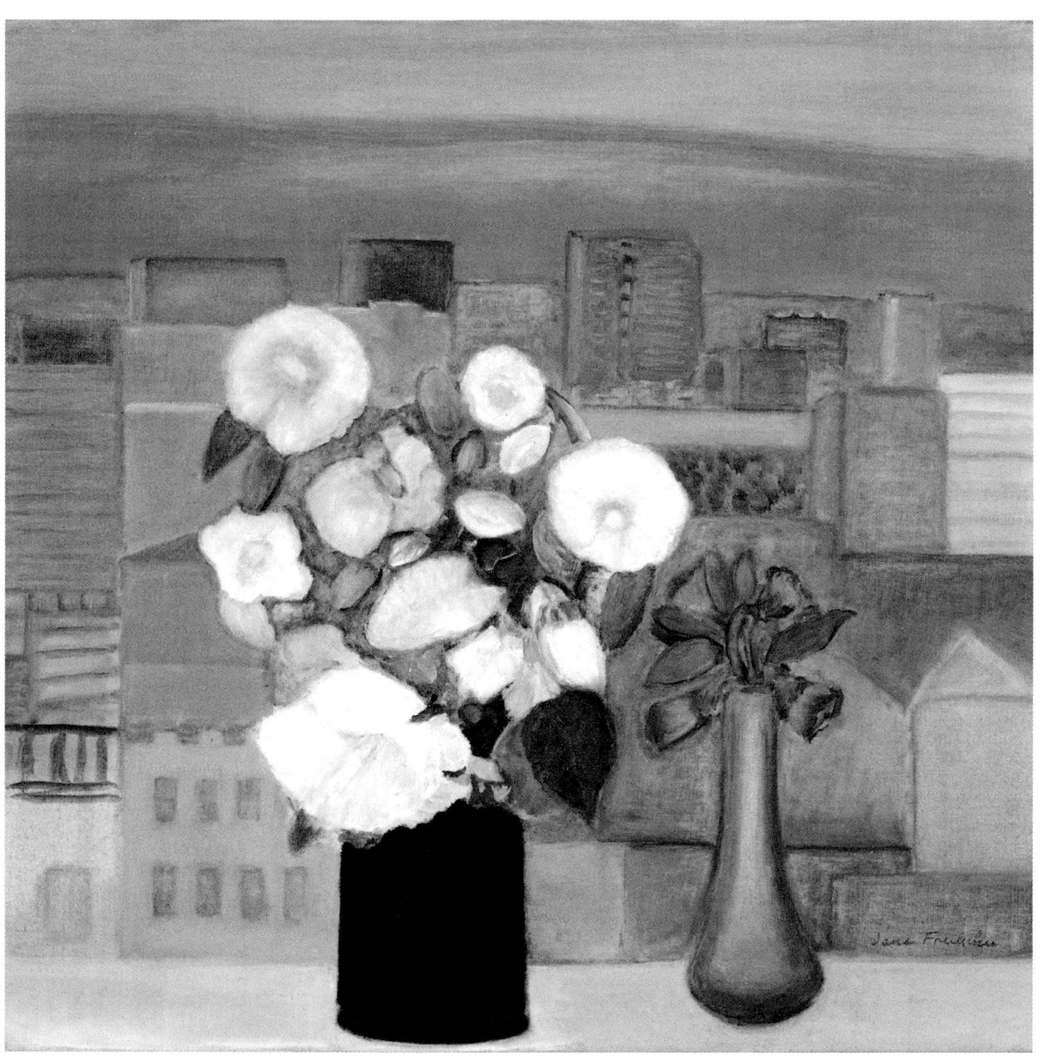

Jane Freilicher
Afternoon in October, 1976
Oil on linen
51 x 77 inches
© Jane Freilicher
Courtesy Tibor de Nagy Gallery, New York

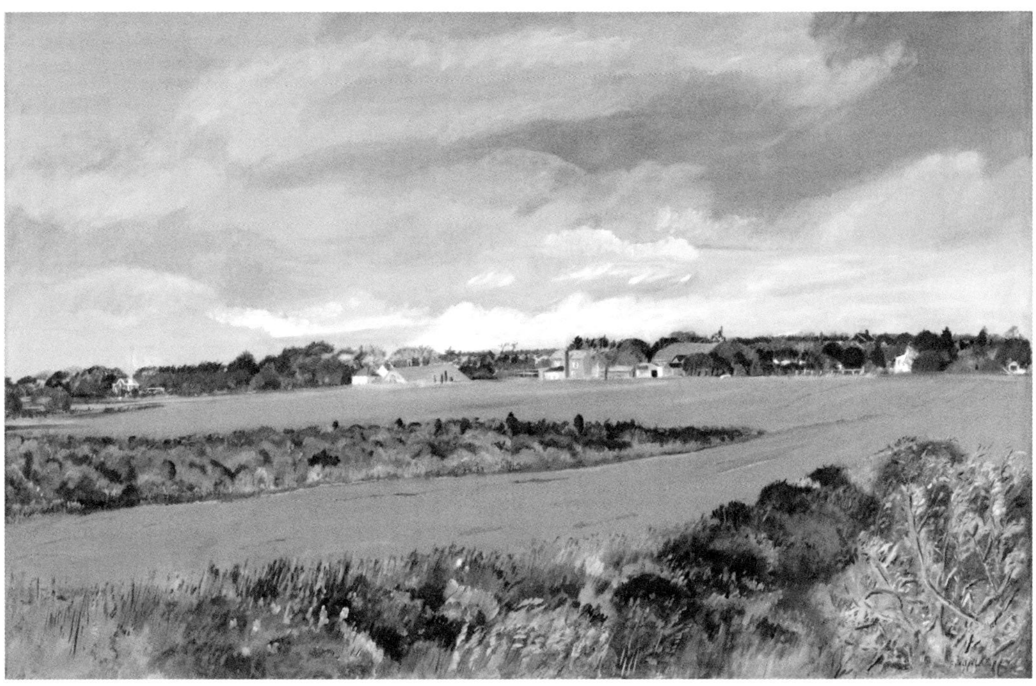

from 1967 is of Jane and her daughter, Elizabeth, when she was just a small child. Here, Jane is sitting and looking directly at her portraitist; she is wearing a short, lilac-colored dress with a pattern on it, and little Elizabeth is wearing red overalls with a pattern as well. It is a touching depiction of mother and child in the Long Island landscape. Jane owned this work and generously gave it to the Parrish Art Museum. It is not only a significant work of Porter's but also a document of the lives and friendship of these two artists. Porter died in 1975 when he was sixty-eight.

In this exhibition of Freilicher's there are eleven works, several from 2012, and all but one is a botanical still life set against the New York cityscape. Freilicher brings the planes of color from the background up close to the surface of the picture and pushes the color of the botanicals in the foreground back to make them combine and flatten. This is Hans Hofmann's technique of "push and pull," which had a tremendous influence on artists of the New York School. Hofmann was an influential painter and teacher with whom Freilicher studied in Provincetown. I studied in graduate school with a group of painters from the next generation who were trained as abstract expressionists but turned away from abstraction to return to figuration. They were influenced by Hofmann, may have studied with Hofmann, and were very good at moving their hands this way or that to describe the space we, the students, were seeing in the set-up or landscape from which we worked. I loved watching this push and pull dance and wondered if Hofmann himself had explicated his ideas with similar gestures.

Where Hofmann's colors vibrate against one another, however, Freilicher's colors sit softly in the same tonal range even as they playfully create spatial tensions. In a small (eight by ten inches) liquid landscape from 2010, the greenish gray in the foreground recedes into coral and yellow and breathes upward into the twilight sky of a grayish blue that comes forward and flattens the picture.

In the paintings Freilicher made on Long Island, the horizon and clear, cloudless sky dominate the compositions. There is often a wonderful swatch of bright and clean cadmium yellow that rakes across the greenest of pastoral grass. Although nominally interiors and landscapes, the true subject of Freilicher's paintings is color and the quiet but very com-

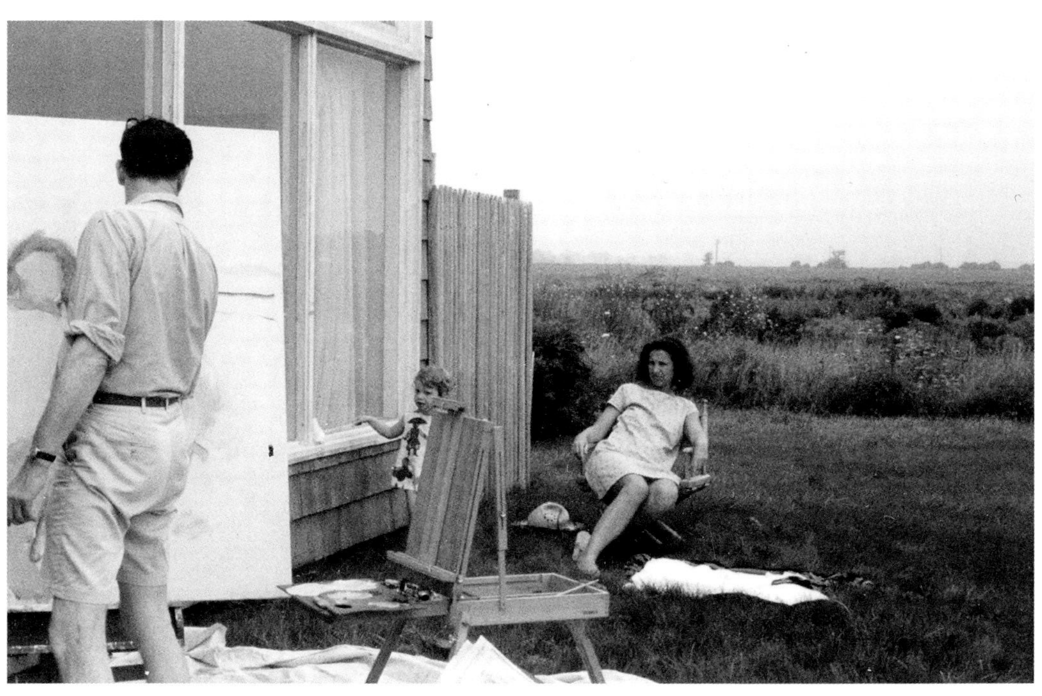

pelling dramas hue can enact. There are no people in these paintings, except as distant, abstract presences.

For over sixty years, Jane has made peaceful paintings that explore the relationship of each form and color, each shape, to the one next to it. Her landscapes are full of flattened yellow shapes that articulate the path of sunshine. It is a particular bright, clean yellow that signifies the Long Island landscape in full summer or autumn sunlight. Paintings like *September Moment* (1998–99) have it, as do other landscapes like *Goldenrod* (1999) or mixed motif works like *Mallows in an Earthenware Jar* (2001). In this painting the yellow is a bit more than halfway down the canvas. Her paintings are like having the sun on one's face after a winter of gray and cold.

Jane's repeated motif is a small and lovely vase of flowers in the foreground of her compositions, innocently arranged on the tabletop to set up the space of the view beyond it. This vase is a compositional device that serves to center the image and create pictorial space. Jane has worked over and over with this motif. It is like a mantra that she speaks quietly, and that the paintings repeat quietly to us.

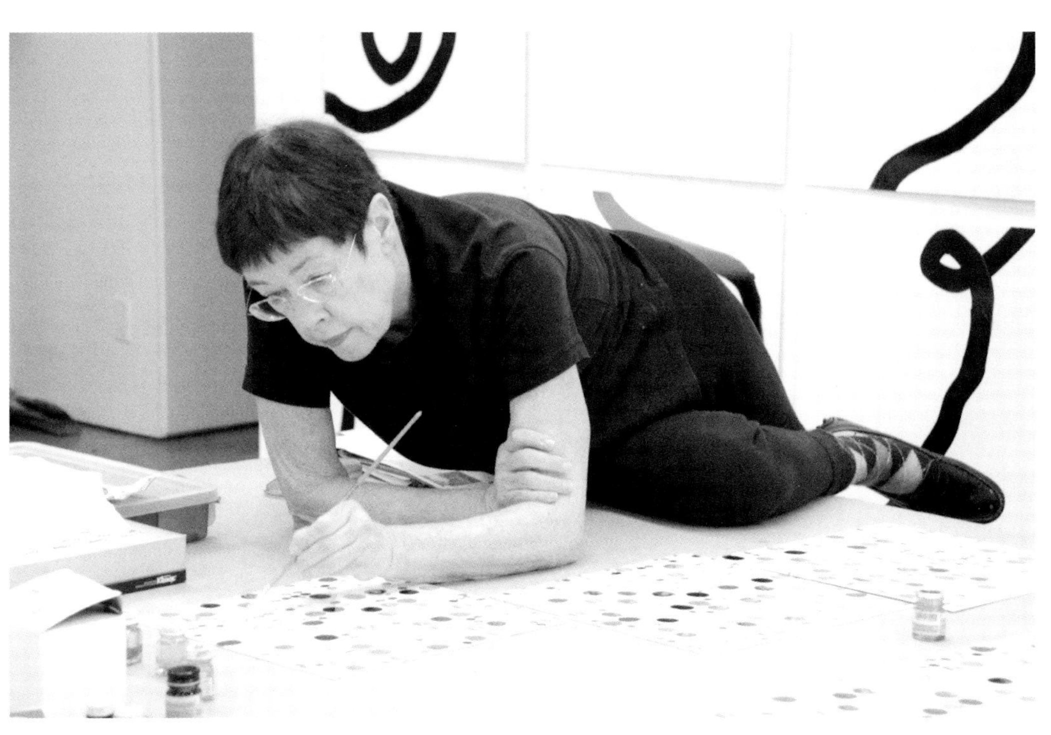

Jennifer Bartlett
Tending the Garden

I

On a drizzly spring morning in 2012 I traveled by subway to the home and studio of Jennifer Bartlett. She had recently moved from Manhattan to the Fort Greene section of Brooklyn, which is becoming increasingly gentrified. I got out of the subway station and immediately fell under the spell of the neighborhood with its large trees and brownstone buildings.

Her long-time assistant greeted me at the door and led me into an airy and well-organized studio with large metal tables at its center. There was a lovely sitting area with a striped daybed and two chairs upholstered in black-and-white patterns with overlapping circular shapes, a design of which I am very fond. When Jennifer came down to greet me she was also dressed in black and white, and when she took a seat on the daybed she looked like she was part of a Matisse composition.

Jennifer and I spoke about her work for a long time, and then she took me on a tour of the garden and the rest of the studio. She is articulate and easy to talk to. She is quick and funny and exudes joie de vivre. Some of her responses seemed designed to encourage me to investigate her work on my own. When I asked about how she begins a work, she said, "I begin the work." What sizes do you work in? "Small, medium, and large." So, I gladly took up the challenge.

Jennifer's pivotal work *Rhapsody* (1975–76), which was on view at the Museum of Modern Art in NYC in 2011, is composed of 987 twelve-by-twelve-inch steel plates painted in baked-on enamel. Each plate is silk-screened with a grid of pale gray that the color brushstrokes sit on and within. These works sit flat on the wall and are arranged in rows of seven so that they are much taller than the viewer and span 147 feet. Each plate contains one of several kinds of images. Some are solid colors or brushy color fields, while others represent landscapes, sky, clouds, or trees. Some are painted representationally. Others are depicted schematically, or in a cartoon-like fashion, or as systems of lines and curves or geometrical shapes. The scale of the work is wonderful, but it is the intimacy of the individual plates that seduces the viewer into staying with the work and reading it from left to right and up and down. Both the reworking of images in different styles and the juxtaposition of monumental and intimate scale are signature contrasts in Jennifer's work.

One of the first books I owned that focused entirely on a woman artist was Jennifer Bartlett's *In the Garden*, published in 1982. I was living in Ithaca, New York, and perhaps still recuperating from graduate school and feeling quite isolated living in a college town while being neither a student nor a professor. I realized later that Ithaca was anything but isolated, but my past living experiences had only been of New York City. Reading this book and looking at the 197 reproductions in it, I journeyed with Jennifer through the process of thinking through a single motif, a view of the garden with no people, just a lush landscape with cypress trees and a reflecting pool with a small statue of a nude boy peeing in the water at the far end. I loved this period of Jennifer's work. As a young artist, I felt a kinship with the idea of being in a lonely place; these works conveyed the feeling of being alone in a lush but forgotten hideaway (actually a house in France, outside of Nice). Each of these numbered drawings and paintings from 1980 is different in its balance between abstraction and representation. The diptych format she chose makes the contrasts and juxtapositions all the more poignant. She draws and paints in watercolor and other media the same motifs over and over again, finding a new language for the garden, pool, and statue each time.

In the first drawing of this series, Jennifer used pencil lines to partition the rectangular sheet of paper into two squares that sit side by side. The left side is fierce, angular, and geometric, while the square on the right is articulated by soft marks that build the composition in a manner that might be considered impressionistic. Turn the page, and the next drawing retains the double square, the double landscape, and the proportions of the first, but a brown pencil has crept in to alter this variation on a theme. By drawings number six and number seven, black ink has joined the pencils.

Jennifer Bartlett
In the Garden Drawing #33, 1980
Pen and ink on paper
9.5 x 26 inches
© Jennifer Bartlett

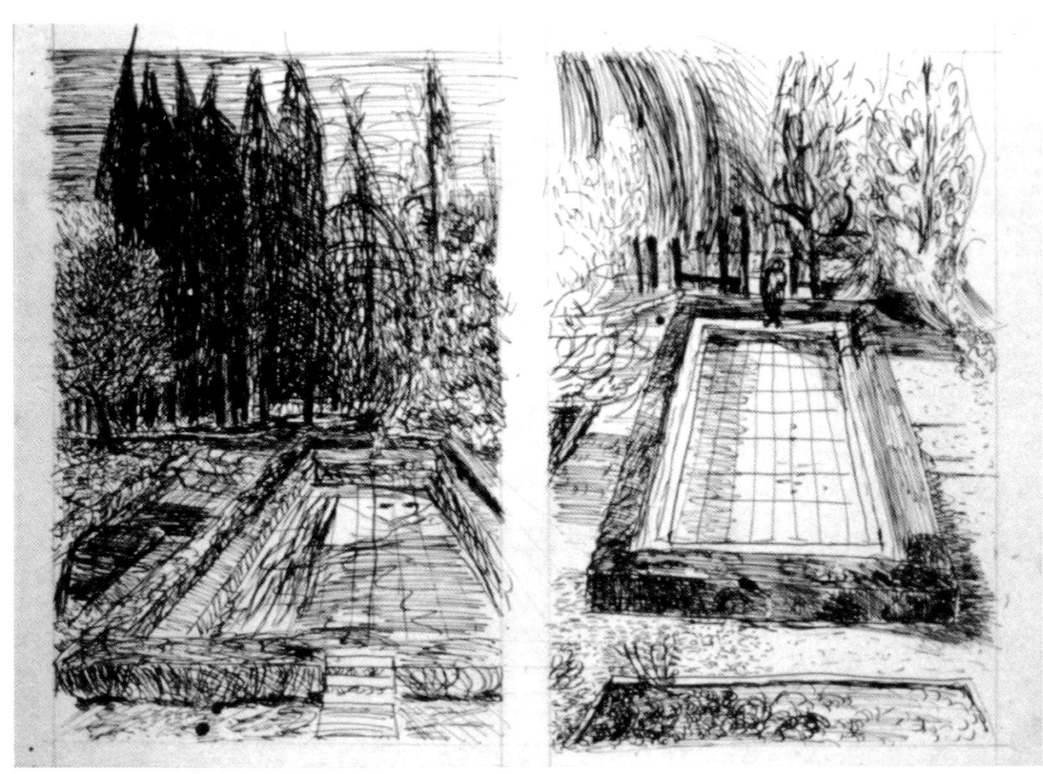

The ink strokes are bolder, more playful, and have a greater presence. By this point in the series, it seems that Jennifer has shaken off any inhibiting rules, and the most beautiful freedom of representation has been let loose on the page. Color arrives with watercolor and then colored pencils. The pool, the light on the water, and the little statue come alive in the medium of gouache, which brings saturated color to the drawings. By drawing number twenty-six, Jennifer has left the frame of the square, and the bold cypress trees at the top of the composition refuse to stay contained. Soon, the drawings grow into two large vertical rectangles that sit side by side and fill the entire page. If this description sounds like a narrative, it is because viewing the works in sequence creates the kind of suspense we experience from movie thrillers. What will happen when we turn the next page?

As we wander around looking at plants and a small water garden, I realize that Jennifer's garden reflects the same aesthetic as these drawings. A Douglas fir is planted beside a tree of a different species to contrast rather than to blend. A long rectangular concrete pool holds water, ready for lilies and other water plants to be cultivated. And beside it, in contrast, is a large natural rock, the right scale to sit upon.

Jennifer came east from California to attend Yale in 1963. She told me she simply wanted to go to the best possible school. At Yale, Jennifer found her particular language of painting, which is representational but also entails the breaking down of all forms to squares, rectangles, and triangles. She embraced the grid. The resulting play of abstraction and representation is evident in a work from 1976, *Falcon Avenue, Seaside Walk, Dwight Street, Jarvis Street, Greene Street*, made up of eighty baked enamel steel plates on a silkscreen grid; the total size is 51 by 259 inches. The motif of this work is a square red house with a triangular black roof set against a blue sky, with a rectangular area of green lawn in front of it. Reading the work from left to right, we first see the house through a veil of white that makes it seem like a distant memory. In the next version, the white is gone, resulting in a more intense image of this schematic representation of home. The next image is pointillist in style, and the house starts to lose definition. The colors begin to mix; black and blue dots run into the sections previously reserved for just red or green or blue. By the fourth group

Jennifer Bartlett
Amagansett Diptych #2, 2007
Oil on canvas
96 x 192 inches
© Jennifer Bartlett

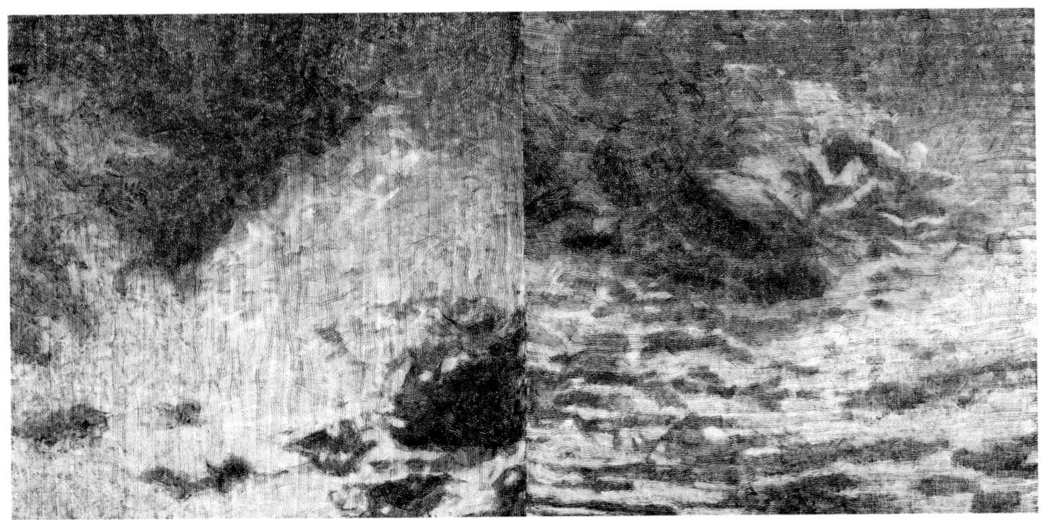

of plates, the brushwork and color have become expressionistic; the basic unit of this image is the stroke rather than the dot, and the work's geometry is no longer regular. In the final image to the far right, the house is no longer identifiable.

The overall movement of the work suggests a trajectory of some kind, expressed in shifts of style and variations in the treatment of the image. It may be autobiographical. Falcon Avenue is a street in Long Beach, California, where Jennifer is from—perhaps the sequence carries her from her origins on the West Coast to her adopted home of Soho, New York, where Greene Street is located. I have always been interested in the stylistic pendulum that swings between representation and abstraction, and particularly in the graceful shifting between them. Rather than treating abstraction and representation as opposites, Jennifer travels back and forth between them, breaking themes down into small elements she can rearrange.

Jennifer told me about her early days as an artist in Soho in the 1960s. Artists were real estate pioneers in their lust for space to make their work. It is hard to believe those lofts were ever filled with a community of artists; it was still a pretty raw place when I started going to galleries there in the mid-1970s. Now it is like an urban mall filled with shops and restaurants and a few galleries. However, the sense of community that originated in the 1970s, anchored by strong friendships among artists, still exists today. I notice a large painting by Elizabeth Murray on the wall. Jennifer sees me looking at it and tells me of their friendship, which lasted through many decades until Murray died of lung cancer in 2007. They met in 1962 when both attended Mills College in California. Jennifer was a senior and Elizabeth a first-year graduate student; they both came east around the same time.

Jennifer also spoke about the day-to-day life of being an artist, something she is matter of fact about: it is simply who she is and what she does. She works in her studio, painting downstairs and drawing upstairs. She is very prolific, making prints, drawings, paintings, and photographs as studies for paintings. This strength, and the will to rise every morning to paint or draw—to create—is powerful. Jennifer does not dwell on it; she just gets to work. I have seen this inner conviction in many great artists. It is there right from the beginning and remains until the end.

The day I visited Jennifer's studio, three of her large studio walls were hung with ten evenly spaced canvases, each forty-eight by forty-eight inches. A twelve-by-twelve-inch photo rested against the wall under each corresponding painting. The paintings were in progress; about half were cityscapes of buildings looking out over the river and the other half were hallways of some institutional space, a doorway or corridor. Jennifer considers the entire group to make up a single series. Upstairs in the drawing studio, as large as the painting studio below though with a lower ceiling, are exquisite pastels of the same views. These images were from Jennifer's hospital stay last year, which we spoke about, but not in depth. It must have been a difficult time for such a lively and productive artist. There is great contrast in these new works, as in all of Jennifer's work, but this time the contrast is in the viewpoint. The cityscapes are seen from a distance, while the institutional hallways are close, abstracted, and eerie. They share the darkness and melancholy of the *In the Garden* series. These works were unfinished when I saw them in May of 2012, so I don't want to say too much about them. They could have changed in myriad ways by now, and I am anxious to see them.

II

I spoke again with Jennifer this afternoon, in February of 2013. I asked about the works that were in process when I saw her last. They have been abandoned for now, so I will not be seeing them any time soon.

When I first met her, Jennifer told me that she thinks of her work as small, medium, and large. Again she told me this, like a sphinx posing an important riddle for me; if I can understand what she meant, I will have the key to opening all the levels of the painting. I am quite sure she does not mean the size of the substrate, although she has made quite a few very large works. The work *Swimmers Atlanta, Seaweed, Flare, Eel* (1981) in the Atlanta Federal Building is two hundred feet in one direction, and the 372 square plates that make up *Recitative* (2009–10) extend to a total of 158 feet. It is made of 372 one-foot-square panels that have been silk-

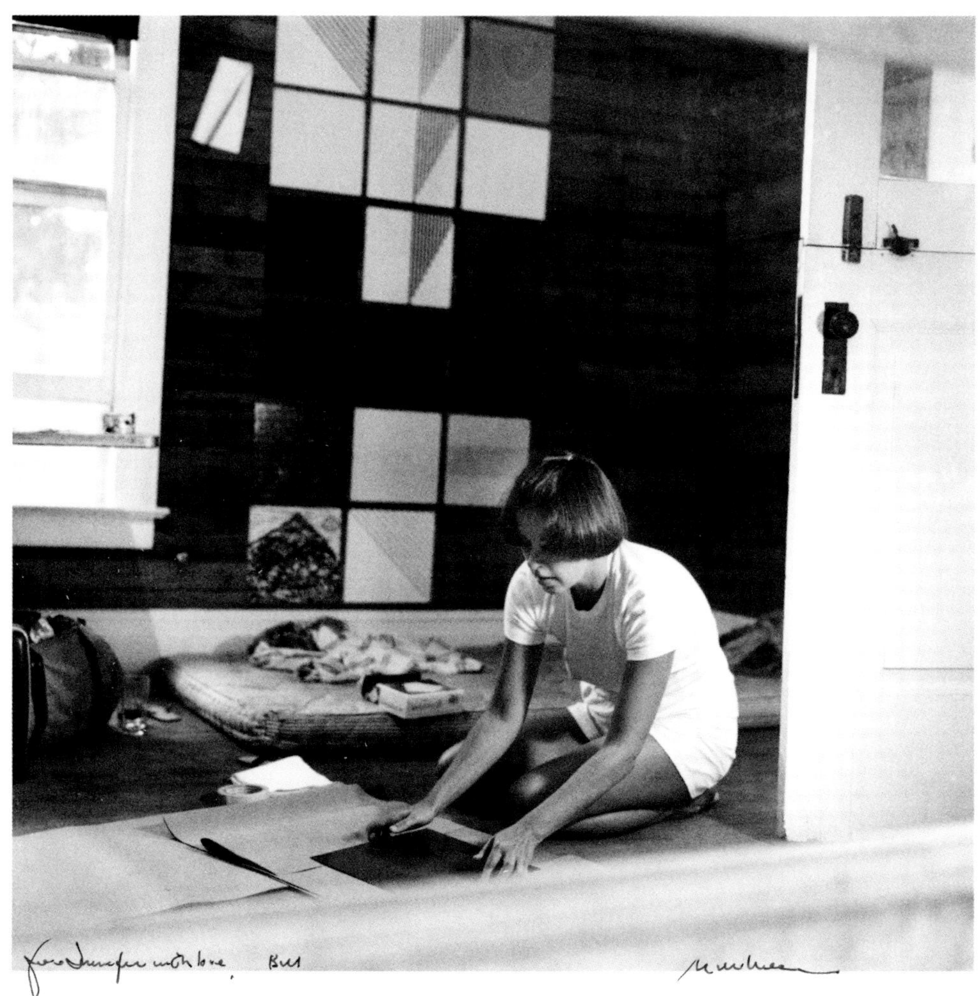

screened with an enamel grid and baked. But I am sure this is not what she is referring to.

If it is not the size of the work that comes in small, medium, or large, then it must be the way Jennifer looks at the object she is painting or drawing and how she breaks it apart. Sometimes the pieces are quite small, resulting in an abstract reading of the object. This process is a bit like zooming in and out—the closer Jennifer's point of view is to the thing she's depicting, the larger it appears. But it also becomes more abstract, because the image breaks down at close range. When we look at a house from very close up, for instance, it becomes a pattern of small dots and dashes. From a more distant perspective, the house retains its visual integrity and the image becomes more referential or representational than abstract.

The paradox is that it is difficult to map small, medium, and large onto different points of view. Is the point of view of an extreme close up large because the object fills the frame? Or is it small because the object breaks down into its constituent parts? The more I look at Jennifer's work, the more I see the process of her painting. I see her mind jump from pointillist dots to lines that ebb and flow. I see a plate of yellow dots that will be joined by other plates of yellow dots to make up the side of a house. This movement between ways of seeing may explain the way she is able to move between representation and abstraction with such fidelity to both seemingly opposite modes.

Going back to Jennifer's *In the Garden* series, I see that it is not the experiment in rendering a single image in different media I thought it was. Rather, it has to do with seeing the same thing over and over again from different perspectives and rearticulating the motif differently each time.

Jennifer works all the time in the studio. It is her life; it is what she does. I love this young picture of her from 1975, taken while she is working. Seeing the world and making art from it is how Jennifer works; she tells us the story of how she sees, and I want to listen.

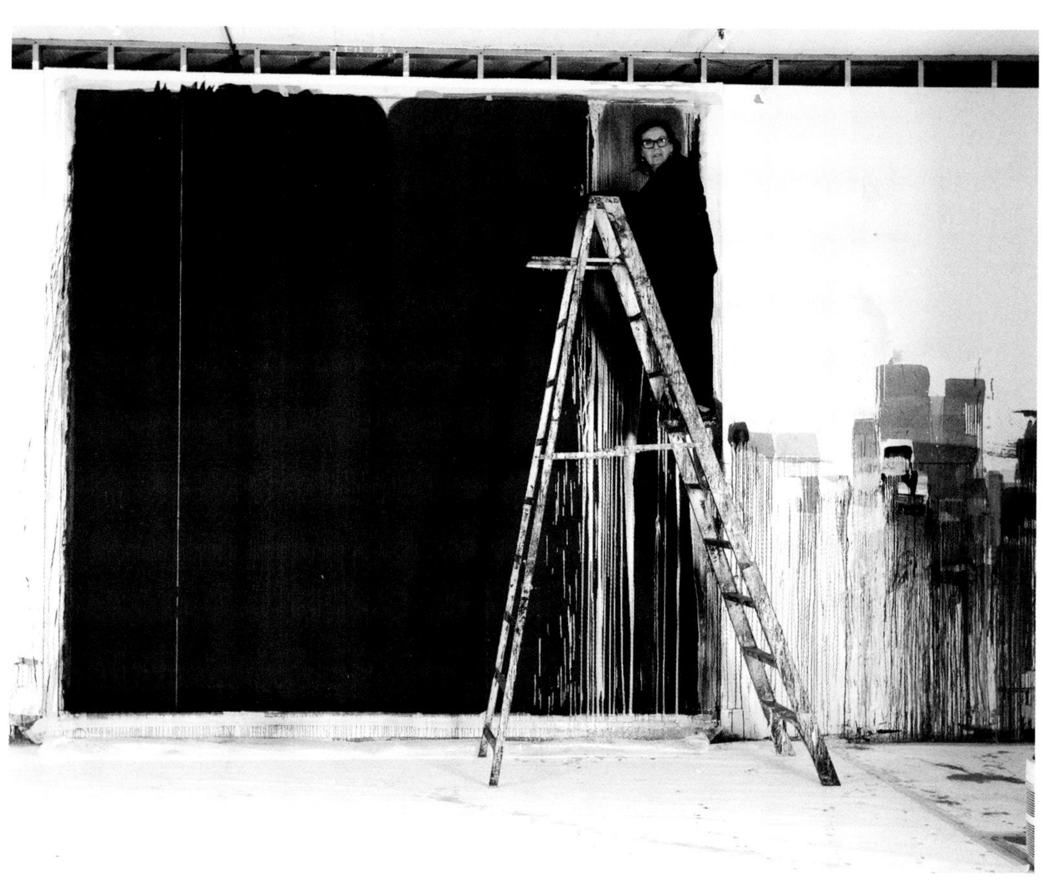

Pat Steir
Art is Life

I

The experience of meeting an artist, of seeing the connection between the physical person and the artwork, can be profound. I met with Pat Steir in September of 2010 in her Chelsea studio, and we chatted about her life as an artist. Her work is huge in scale; yet, she is so attuned to the physical process that requires her to climb ladders or scaffolding to make her work that it seems effortless. Well known for her work since the 1970s, her first museum exhibition was in a group show at the High Museum in Atlanta in 1963. Her life, which is all about being able to work and make paintings, is her art. Pat found a kindred spirit in her friend the painter Agnes Martin (who died in 2004) when she visited her in New Mexico. "For Agnes, art was life and life was art. This was a great inspiration to me."

Stapled to the wall in Steir's studio are six new paintings in very early stages of completion, each twelve feet tall. Seeing these sneak previews of works to come provides unique insight into the paintings. There is a tall ladder for the artist to climb up and down on while painting, a physically demanding task that Steir tackles tirelessly. The painting closest to the window is made up of dark shades of a warm green that turn almost blue against a warm version of a mixed green that will serve as an underlayer for the color to be applied next. The first few layers are very liquid and made from layers upon layers of transparent paint that are poured over each other. The studio columns are adorned with Steir's signature drips, where she has tested some beautiful, metallic hues of pigment and medium to see how each combination might affect the drip. When I asked about painting on huge canvases versus painting on ones the length of her arms, Steir surprised me by saying that she does not prefer one over the other but simply considers them to be different.

Pat Steir, 2012
Photo: Rebecca
Robertson

Steir's studio has been extremely busy of late, but I think she is not one to let her works sit idle. She has made more than fifty wall paintings around the world, agreeing to take on such commissions whenever she has the chance. These works are responsive to their architectural settings, though the architecture can be an adversary rather than a partner, as was the case in her show at the Cincinnati Contemporary Arts Center, whose building was designed by Zaha Hadid. Steir's monumental installation, *Water and Stone* (2010), juxtaposed rigidly gridded austere walls stained with sixteen layers of indigo and black paint with splashes and drips of white paint, evoking waterfalls, splashes of water, and celestial bodies. In a video of the piece's installation, one can see Steir atop scaffolding painting directly onto the dark wall. Her hand touches the black wall with her brush, which is laden with very liquid white paint that ever so eloquently drips and slides down the wall. In this installation, Steir employs some of the motifs—such as waterfalls and more graphic minimal drawing—that have preoccupied her for years.

Four other shows of Steir's work opened in 2010, including *Pat Steir: Drawing Out of Line*, which opened at the Rhode Island School of Design Museum and traveled to the Neuberger Museum at Purchase College, State University of New York. This show focuses on four distinctive bodies of drawings Steir has made over the past thirty-five years. In conjunction with this exhibit, a team of thirty students from the college is recreating *Self-Portrait: An Installation* (1987), a large-scale wall drawing of eyes, noses, and mouths rendered in the manner of Renaissance anatomical studies. As if all this were not enough, Steir had exhibitions both in Paris at Galerie Jaeger Bucher from October 2010 through January 2011 and at Cheim & Read Gallery in New York City in February and March of 2011. At Sue Scott Gallery on Rivington Street in New York City, Steir unfolded an immersive site-specific installation transforming both rooms of the gallery into what she describes as a "nearly endless line" from early November 2010 through early January 2011.

Pat Steir has been important to me as a painter since I first saw her work in the Virginia Museum in Richmond in the early 1980s when she developed her painting motif by dissecting Brueghel still lifes into gridded, mural-sized works. In each square of the grid she made a painting that

Pat Steir
White Splash on Black, Black Splash on White, 2009
Oil on canvas
84 x 84 inches
© Pat Steir
Courtesy Cheim & Read Gallery, New York

constituted her response to the corresponding area of the original painting "in the style of an historical painter that the space brought to mind." Each square was different. Collectively, they added up to a very large work in a collection of styles and colors. I could not help but enjoy these monumental post-modernist pastiches—the painting as a wikipedia of styles. She took over the master's painting, and she owned it.

The Brueghel Series (A Vanitas of Style) (1982–4) represented a postmodern turn in Steir's work. In the 1970s, her work had been abstract. Her paint handling was gestural, but her compositions were discontinuous, often broken down into discrete elements. She then proceded to a series of works about color and mark making. Currently it is her relationship to nature that is extremely compelling. Her gestural drips and splashes of paint now read as weather, as waterfalls, as water, as the oceans climbing up the shore. Steir can change water into fire or tree limbs with a flick of the color wheel. There is a bit of magic going on here, magic that derives from the necessary relationship between nature and humanity. As Steir puts it, "We are all the shape of nature, our inner sound, our heartbeat, is the rhythm of the universe, for sure. What else can it be? Sometimes we're in contact with it and sometimes we're not. I think this is what Pollock meant when he said, 'I am nature.'"

As I leave Steir's studio, she hands me a heavy book on her work published in 2006. On the cover is an image from *Venice Veils: A Dream Project* (1999) in which a Venetian façade is rendered ethereal by being glimpsed through waterfalls. The impossible artworks that make up this project are fascinating: splashes of water and drips fall down over Venetian archways and under bridges.

I find Steir's dream fascinating; she is forever thinking of what the work can or cannot be and pushing beyond the physical limits of painting.

II

It is early in the year, just a couple of weeks into 2013, and Pat and I catch up. The body of work Pat was preparing when I visited her studio

Pat Steir
Twenty-One Musicians on a White Elephant, 1991
Oil on canvas
173 x 115 inches
© Pat Steir
Courtesy Cheim & Read Gallery, New York

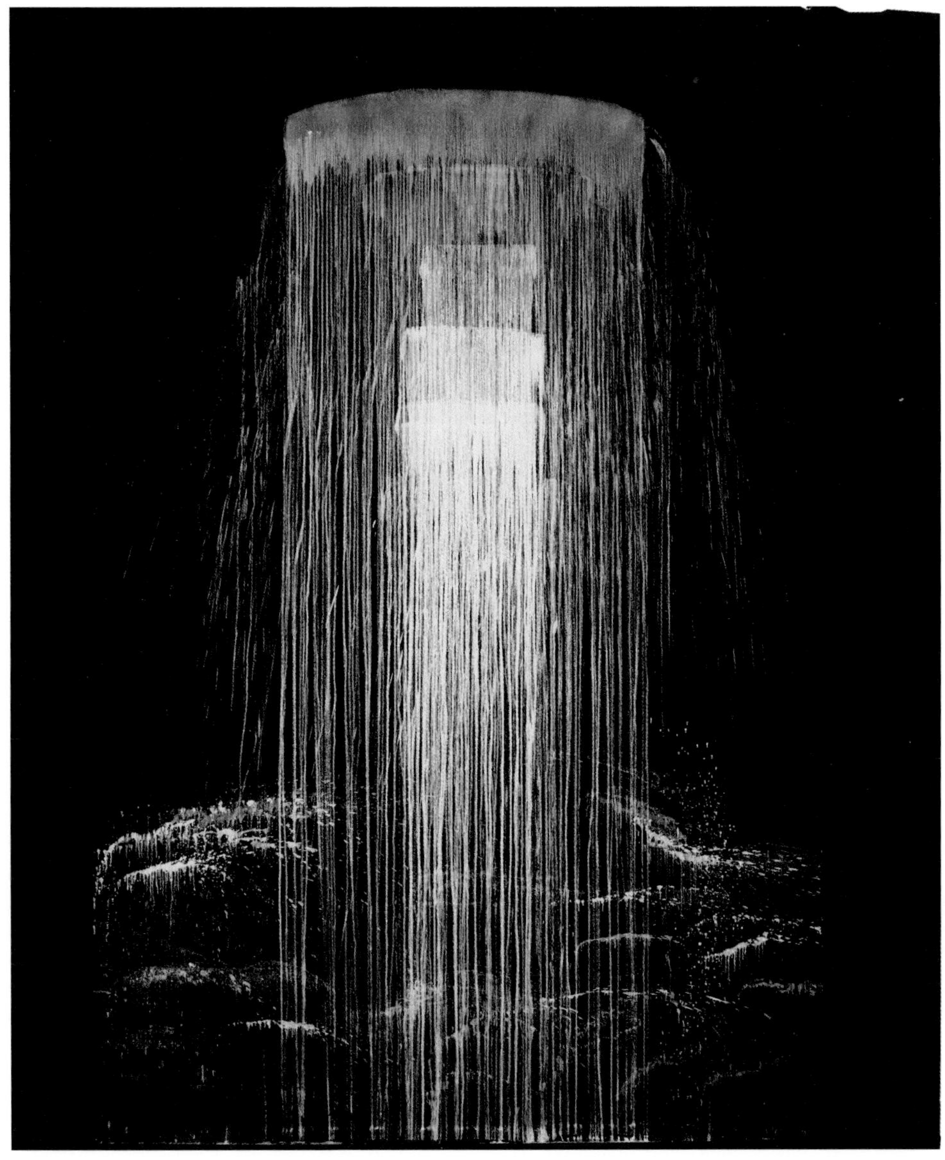

has since been shown at Cheim & Read, a gallery in the Chelsea neighborhood of New York City. In March, Pat is going to have a large exhibition she is very excited about, in Mexico City at the Museo Nacional de San Carlos. It is a glorious museum filled with European art and wonderful spaces where Pat is planning to show both wall work and installations.

She has just moved studios and is exhausted from the process, although she tells me she did not do the actual moving. I understand this completely; a studio move for an artist is discombobulating, but also can be exhilarating. Pat tells me she is happy with the new studio; it is in the same building as before, but has a better painting space. Her work, which is not normally stored in her studio anyway, will be stored just a few blocks away in a building that specializes in artists' works. Having your art storage separate from your workspace is bliss for any artist, and with Pat's enormous canvases it must be even more so. For this new studio, she finally bought a lift so that she can work up and down on her paintings with no one else in the studio. Pat needs to be able to be at the top of her paintings to make the aqueous waterfalls and veils of intensely hued oil paint that pour down the thirteen feet of the painting.

I did not make it to Pat's opening at Cheim & Read, but I saw the show when there were fewer people in the gallery. The paintings command a lot of attention and demand surrounding quiet. The show was called *Winter Paintings* and consisted of twelve large-scale works, each filling a wall of the gallery. The compositions of all but two are almost split down the middle. They have a huge presence.

These magnificent works of art bring to mind the amazing way large-scale paintings can surround you, like nature. The stark vertical split of the canvas in these works is a bit like turning the world ninety degrees when looking at the ocean or another clear horizon. You get the feeling that you are in the work, like when I see one of Claude Monet's paintings of water lily ponds in the Orangerie or the giant fountain-like splash of a Morris Louis. There is something of Mark Rothko in these paintings as well, in the way each color has a dynamic conversation with the color next to it. There is a sensation of air, color, and light in each of these works. Each is so powerful that, as a viewer, I want to soak up their essence through quiet meditation.

The paintings are named for colors. I am drawn to *Dark Green, Red and Silver* (2009–10). The composition is sliced down the center, like a black-and-white cookie. The left side is painted in a dark but luminous green, the color of forests and the blackness of an ocean at night. The right side is awash in silver over green, the silver and gray being more active than the green. But do not think these works are simple color pairings; there is nothing simple about them. They are made of layer upon layer of wash and oil that have been brushed or thrown onto the canvas and bleed into and onto an image the size of a wall. The silver and green side is like a winter walk just before sunset. In the southern part of the United States there are many winter days when the light is quite even with no direct sunshine, the gray sky bracketed by pine trees; on such days the light can become luminous.

Another work from the show, *Yellow Gold Red Gold* (2009–10), is the tiniest bit off square in the same way these works are the tiniest bit off center. The left side is a shimmering of gold on gold that bleeds down from the top left. The right side is a mixture of many layers of stain with a lovely splatter of gold on top. The dividing line down the middle of the canvas is soft and slightly curved; it is the line discovered by the hand in the course of making the painting rather than by measurement. This regal painting has the presence of a coronation robe or garment for royalty. Pat has translated the scale and power of her waterfall installations into these large paintings.

In thinking about these works I wonder about Pat's friendship with Agnes Martin. Pat met Agnes on a trip west and found in her not just a friend, but someone she could learn from and understand. I came to Agnes's work late; it was not until I saw a show of her then recent work in 1997 at Pace Gallery that I came to understand much about her work. It was one of those amazingly cold New York days in February. It was so cold as I walked to the gallery that my eyes watered, and the wind was so strong it whipped around the buildings and blew right into me. There were very few people out. The first gallery I came to was Pace, and I thought, okay, it is a Martin show, maybe I will see something I had not seen before, maybe I will understand. When the elevator opened, a world of light, passion, and nature opened up to me in those very minimal paintings of

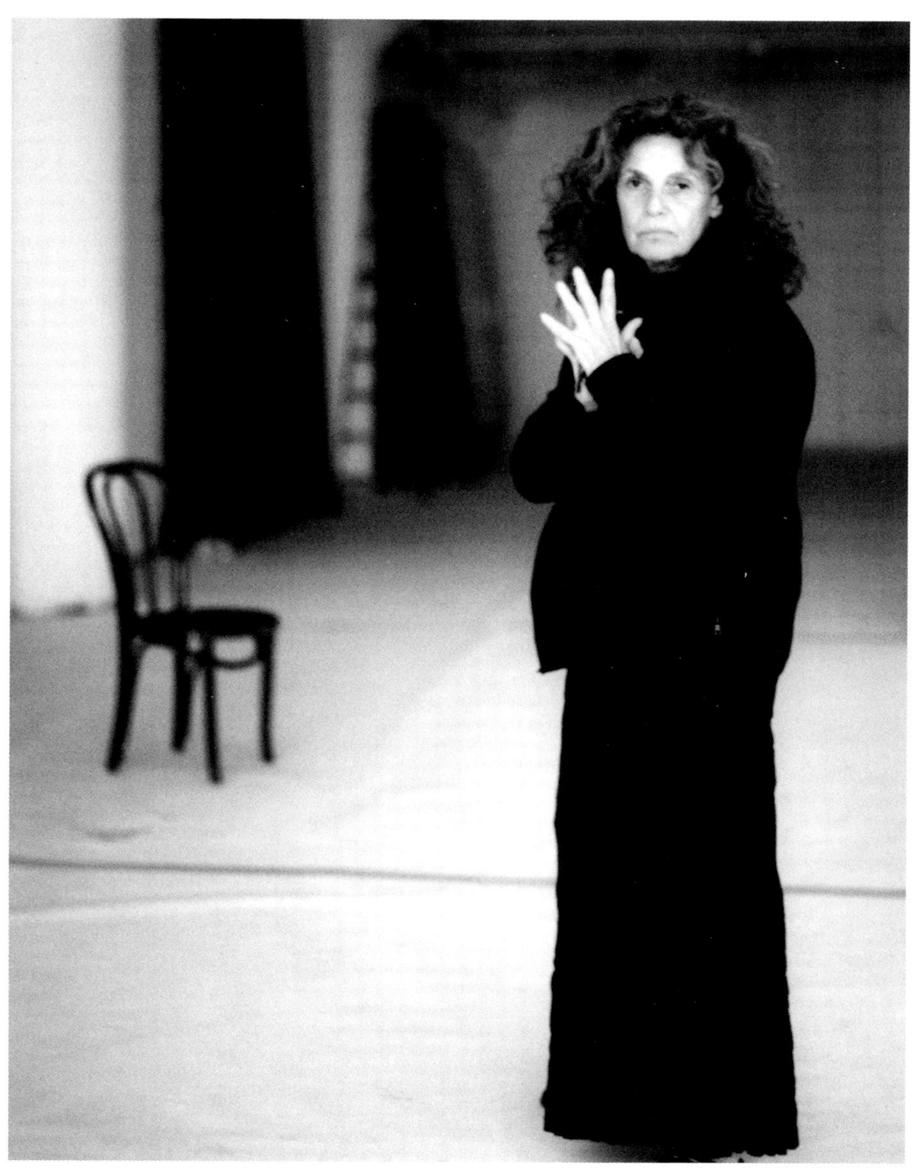

pencil lines and the thinnest paint in blue, gray, or yellow bands of color across the surface. So strongly did I feel the artist's presence, her hand as it moved across the canvas, that I experienced intimacy and such warmth and emotion. I felt the sun on my face and joy in the work.

Pat understood this aspect of Agnes immediately and was drawn to her as a friend. She visited her every year for thirty years and stayed at her home. Their work was in dialogue: both started with the grid and then veered off and out into the opening space of the canvas. For both, the subject is painting, the idea is painting, and the thing is painting.

I think about the travels Pat has taken on her journey as an artist. In 1984, she deconstructed Brueghel by breaking down a bouquet of flowers from one of his paintings on an eight-by-eight grid with each square at a different level of abstraction and representation. Thirty years later, she is opening up the brushstroke in accord with the philosophy of her colleague, the composer John Cage, whom she admired with fondest friendship and deep respect. Cage emphasized the importance of chance and happenstance in the creation of art. Chance is now in the work, as Pat flicks her brush at the wall. I remember watching her pour the small cups of paint thinned with turpentine that melt into the colors underneath them. Pat has moved from the thoughtful, conceptual deconstruction of the mark to an ecstatic saturation of poured splashes of veiled color put down layer upon layer.

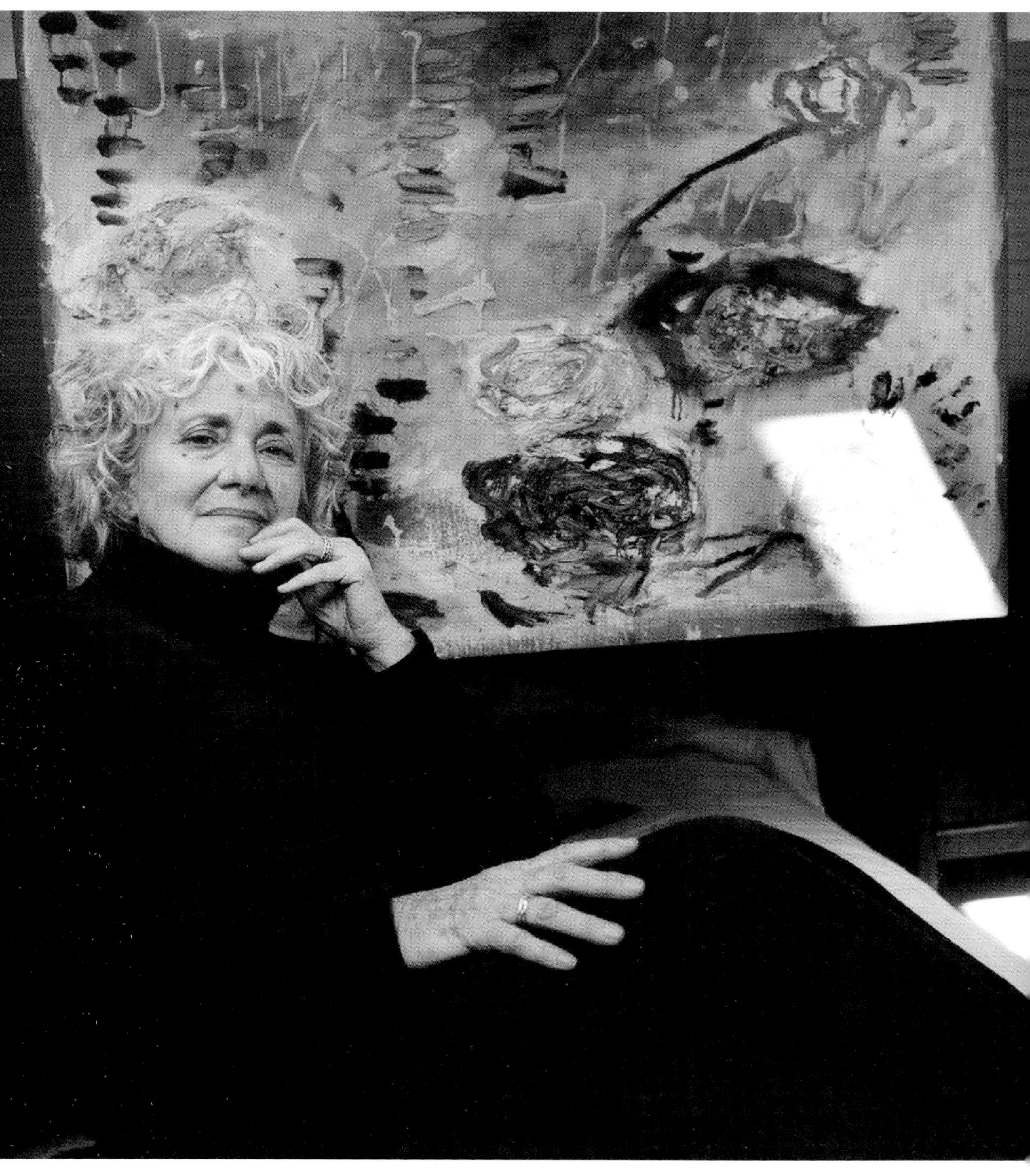

Joan Snyder
Getting It Right

I

In a blue and white house with a studio converted from a carriage house behind it, I found Joan Snyder about to finish lunch with her assistant. The large kitchen possessed the warmth of a place where many meals had been prepared, eaten, and lingered over. We chatted a bit while they finished, and I spent my time gazing upon a resonant horizontal painting of sunflowers, its thick paint massed on the surface with the presence and panache that make Joan's work so distinctive. Gardens figure prominently in Joan's paintings, and later that day she tells me of the summer place with a large garden built by her son-in-law in Woodstock, New York, where she and her partner spend half the year. While telling me of their home in Woodstock, Joan's entire face—no, her entire being—brightens with a delightful smile and a posture that speaks of her happiness while there.

Joan was born and raised in New Jersey. She has white curly hair and wears black round glasses on her intelligent, vibrant face. She speaks with a straightforwardness that I feel comfortable with, maybe because I recognize her clear hard shell as similar to my own demeanor. I know this manner for what it is: it is not hardness, but just a directness that many New Yorkers have. I forget how much I miss it until I experience it again.

We leave the house and take a few steps past a small koi pond that Joan tells me was there when she and her partner bought the house. Her studio is light and airy; the top floor was removed during the conversion to give it a high ceiling and skylights. Joan tells me about her paintings and the books she has been reading for her reading group. She is cavalier with the books; she writes in them and cuts them out of their bindings so that "they will be easier to read in bed." But her recklessness is that of someone who loves books and wants to understand every word and phrase.

Portrait of Joan
Snyder, 2007
Photo: Marni
Majorelle

75

Knowing how she uses books is a delightful way to understand Joan's paintings and how she makes them. She paints colors and forms, covers them over and reveals them. She crosses some images out and brings others up to the surface.

Shown in New York in the fall of 2010 as part of her solo show "A Year in the Painting Life" at Betty Cunningham Gallery, the fondly titled work *Summer Fugue* (2010) is a triptych. The left-hand painting is small and intense, full of bright blooming flowers with an elliptical shape at its center. The taller, yellow-hued center panel is an explosion of flowers. And finally the last panel, small again, is a dark ending to an otherwise brightly colored painting. The paintings are truly mixed media. They incorporate oil and acrylic paint, seeds and herbs, rosebuds and sparkles, burlap and silk. This and other works have dirt, papier-mâché, and cord or rope applied to their surfaces. When she allows parts of the unbleached linen to appear through her rumble of paint and media, they do not read as empty white space. Rather, the linen's tawny color becomes part of the painting's hue.

I spent a long time at this exhibition trying to understand how Joan got it all so right. I started to think about what makes her painting different from those of the thousands of painters who paint fields of flowers. Her paintings are just this side of sweet and nostalgic without ever actually becoming so. If anything, they are tough works with content and soul, like those of her male contemporaries like Kiefer or Rauschenberg. Her work has an uncanny physicality that is built up on the surface with paint. Not only do I have the urge to touch them like doubting Thomas with St. Sebastian's wounds, I want to pierce the surface with my finger and touch the interior of the wound or flower or other orifice.

In the 1960s and 1970s Joan was known for something called "stroke" paintings. The strokes in these large paintings are big marks that move horizontally and vertically on the canvas. Many of the paintings are quilt-like because of their gridded structures and the freshness of their color.

Joan spoke to me about the influence of many types of music on her painting; a recorder and sheet music are on a stand in her studio. Sound is important; not just sound but the rhythms of music whether Eastern or Western, jazz or classical. We talked about how she loves making prints; she will make a print whenever anyone invites her to do so. We talked a

Joan Snyder
Symphony IV, 1977
Oil, fabric, paper, glitter on canvas
60 x 120 inches
© Joan Snyder

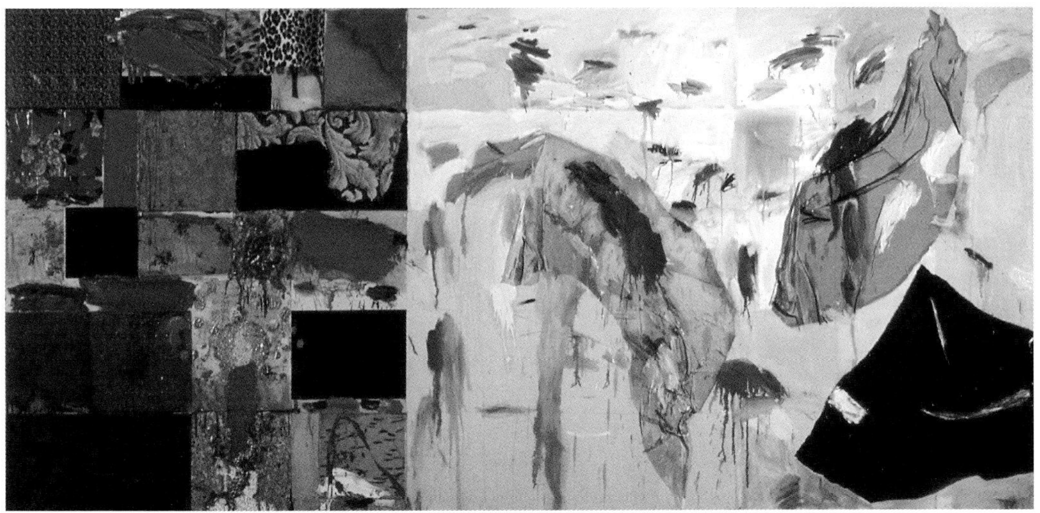

bit about her parents, her middle-class New Jersey childhood, the New York art community, and her relationships with art dealers. Joan also explained that while some aspects of an artist's life may become easier over time, others never do. "My life got easier financially and in other ways. Life in the studio can still be rigorous and sometimes a struggle, [and] dealing with the art world never gets easier!"

She brought out two white paintings that she was finishing. *Still* is a work of layers of different tones of white laid over previously painted areas so that the drips have a wonderful variation of hue behind them. In an impasto of paint are small, round fleurettes in rose, coral, pink, and white. The word "still" is written four times in paint on the surface. Joan tells me that she writes words on canvases when she needs them, when the painting calls for them. "Still" is the perfect word in this case. It is a tribute to her persistence: after all, Joan is *still* making paintings after all these years! But more important is Joan's ability to find a place of mental stillness so that she can make her art.

II

On a quiet Saturday winter morning in 2013 I spoke with Joan. What has changed since we spoke last? Joan and her longtime partner have gotten married this past summer, as same-sex marriage is finally legal in the State of New York. And Joan has become a grandmother, a very special and delightful life event. Joan has had exhibitions at two New York City galleries this past year, Gering & López and Cristin Tierney.

The exhibition at Gering and López looked both forward and back. Pairing recent paintings with works on paper from the late 1960s and early 1970s, the show reveals how much the artist is still involved with the same ideas and motifs and how they have evolved into the recent and larger oil paintings. *Spring Eternal*, an oil on linen work from 2012, is a delicious birthday cake of a painting in which Joan uses mostly white to create the grid that seems to be present to some degree in the work of every mature artist who lived and worked through the 1960s and 1970s.

Joan Snyder
Still, 2011
Oil, acrylic, papier-mâché, twigs, glass
beads, cheesecloth, silk, burlap, rosebuds
on linen
48 x 63 inches
© Joan Snyder
Courtesy of the artist

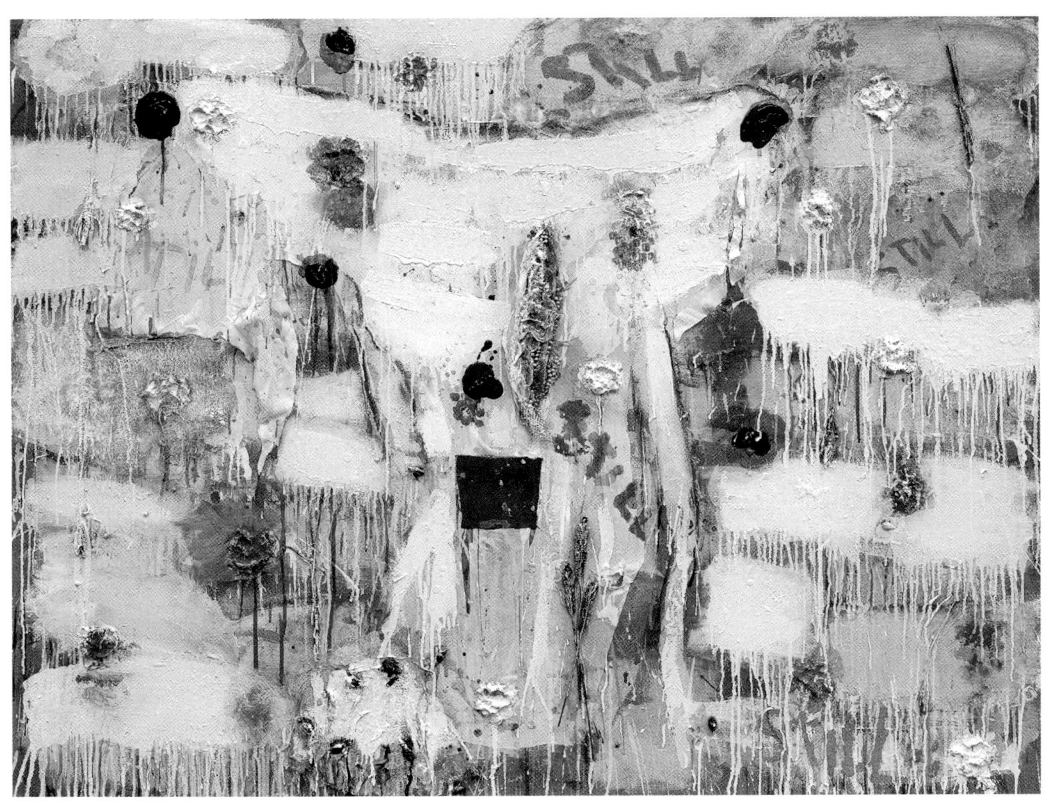

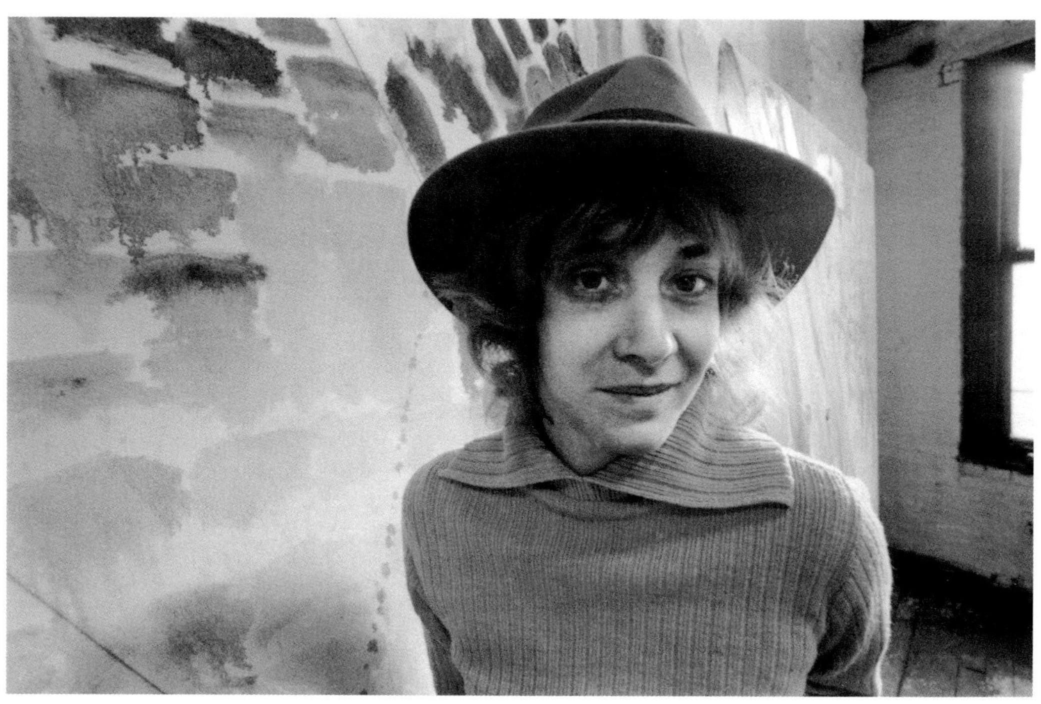

In this painting, Joan hangs bold, intense passages on the grid like laundry. In the upper left there is a patch of bluish purple sky and on the far right is a yellow cloud-like form that pours down yellow hue like rain running down and behind the other marks.

Off center is a large white vulva form with dashes and flecks of paint in thalo green, white, yellow, and rose, contained in a pentimento of paint just peeking through. Combined in the same painting we have bare linen, thick and textural papier-mâché, oil, and acrylic paint. The painted rectangles make one think of garden plots newly planted with seeds. It is a rich and dazzling work.

In 1972, Joan made a 17.5-by-30-inch drawing in oil on paper titled *Screams and Whispers*. Here, the patches and strokes are less organized, there is no grid, but caressing and crossing the page in a slightly curvilinear fashion are several marks to which all the other strokes seem to relate. Unlike *Spring Eternal*, Joan's grid is there only as the faintest presence. Four lines, thicker than the rest, undulate in soft curves that do not cross. It is interesting to watch the grid ebb and flow in these works and then disappear altogether into a drapery-like softness.

Joan paints things we know: sunflowers, meadows, hearts, and flowers. They never turn sweet or sappy. My mother used to tell me I was like a Mallomar, a type of cookie made of marshmallow covered in a hard chocolate: soft on the inside but hard on the outside. I didn't take offense at this description; I heard it for many years and came to identify with it. I wonder if Joan is a bit like this as well. How is she able to keep her work from becoming fluff, even while using dried flowers and velvet? The toughness of her painting always wins out over its sweetness. *Break In Two My Heart* (2011) is a good example: there are passages of sweet pink, but the roughness of the paint handling produces a kind of heaviness that eschews sentimentality. It is much like humidity in the air; you can't really see it but you definitely feel it.

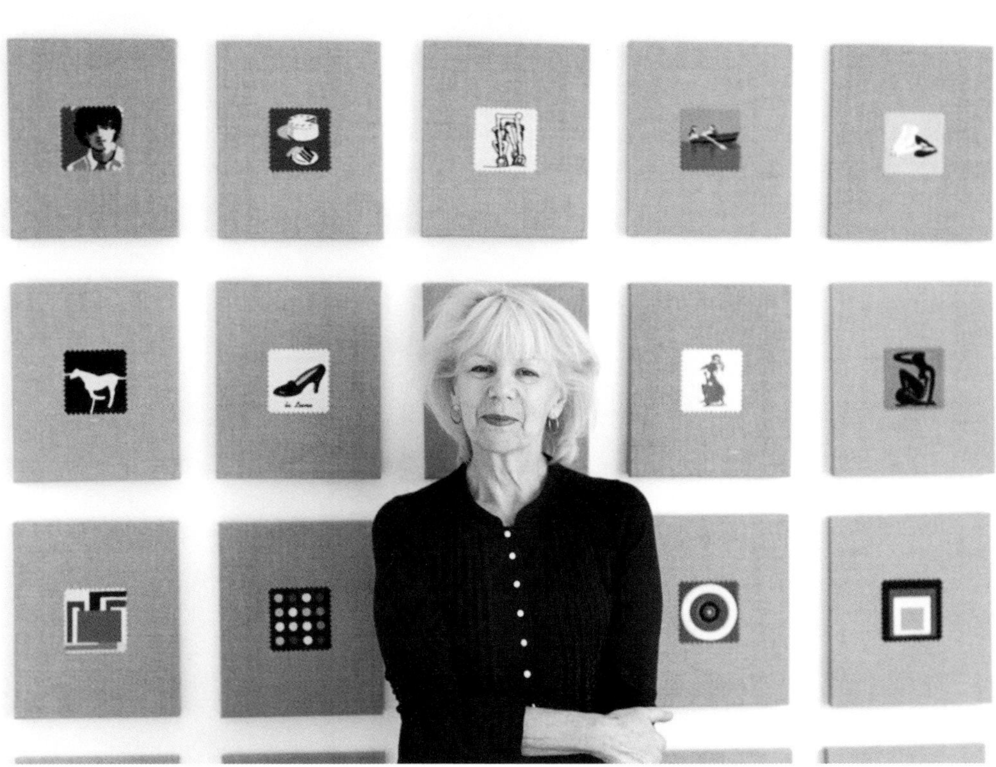

Elaine Reichek
The Thread

I

On a bright Sunday morning I took a bus uptown to Harlem where I visited the New York home and studio of Elaine Reichek. After spending so much time with her work, I would finally meet the artist. As I entered her light-filled home, I was immediately taken with the works displayed on the walls and tables. She brought me iced coffee, chocolate pizzelle cookies and large, delicious crackers. We chatted about her life while sitting on her deck in the sunshine. The beauty of her home and work matched her own elegance and hospitality.

We discovered that we went to the same high school in Brooklyn, although not at the same time. I laughed later when I thought of the other great women who graduated from James Madison High School, including Ruth Bader Ginsburg and Carole King. I like to think there is something in the water there that made us different, in the same way that people will say a given place makes better bread because of the local water. Anyway, unbeknownst to us, we had shared the same streets and hallways and stops on the D train. For me, there is a strange comfort in knowing we once occupied the same longitude and latitude.

Scanning through the many things to see in her home, my eyes were drawn to a small grid of embroidered squares made in reference to Josef Albers's *Homage to the Square*, part of Elaine's "Pattern Recognition" series of 2006–7. Albers, a German-American artist who had been part of the Bauhaus before immigrating to the United States, had served as head of the art department at Yale where Elaine studied, albeit after Albers's retirement. Albers made a series of works with multiple squares nested inside one another based on his theory of color relationships. Elaine's versions are small, jewel-like stamps that replicate Albers's famous nest-

Elaine Reichek in front of *Swatches: B&W 1–25*, 2007
Photo: Paul Kennedy
© Elaine Reichek
Courtesy of Nicole Klagsbrun Gallery, New York
and Shoshana Wayne Gallery, Santa Monica

ing squares of color, only instead of being painted they were made on a digital embroidery machine. They have zigzag edges that look as though they were cut with pinking shears to emulate the look of swatches used for selecting fabrics and matching colors. The pinking shear-like zigzag is especially amusing because these sewing scissors were created to stop woven fabric from unraveling, something neither painting nor digital embroidery does.

I read Elaine's appropriation of Albers as a feminist gesture, particularly since she renders his painted images in the traditionally feminine form of embroidery. Additionally, the fact that she used a digitally driven production method instead of stitching them by hand, as she had done in earlier work, telescopes a history of image-making technologies that encompasses the paint brush, the embroidery hoop, the mechanical embroidery machine and the computer. There is also a playfulness in the way these works blur distinctions between ideas of art and craft (by replicating Albers's art in a medium usually thought of as craft). This is singularly appropriate in light of the work's implied connection with the Bauhaus and its philosophy of uniting fine art and craft, as seen in the work of Albers's wife, Anni, an artist who designed fabrics and made pictorial weavings and collages.

Elaine's work has been informed by her interest in pattern and design since the early 1970s when she first started sewing her art. She felt she needed a different playing field from her male artist colleagues at Yale, who I can imagine took up all the space in the discourse around painting. A bit later, she also made a series of knitted works; she started using embroidery in the early 1990s. There is a strong conceptual element to her work—frequently based on appropriated imagery that Elaine researches extensively—that often centers on contrasts between different modes and means of representation. She works in series, sometimes pursuing the possibilities inherent in a particular set of images and ideas for several years. From the early 1980s through the early 1990s, she used ethnographic photographs of "native" dwellings, Fuegians, and Native Americans as starting points. In these and other works, she reproduced the original photographs but altered them through hand-painting. Certain elements such as the painted body were emphasized or inverted, partly to

Elaine Reichek
Ariadne's Lament, 2009
Digital embroidery on linen
27.5 x 26.5 inches
Photo: Paul Kennedy
© Elaine Reichek
Collection of the Museum of Fine Arts,
Boston

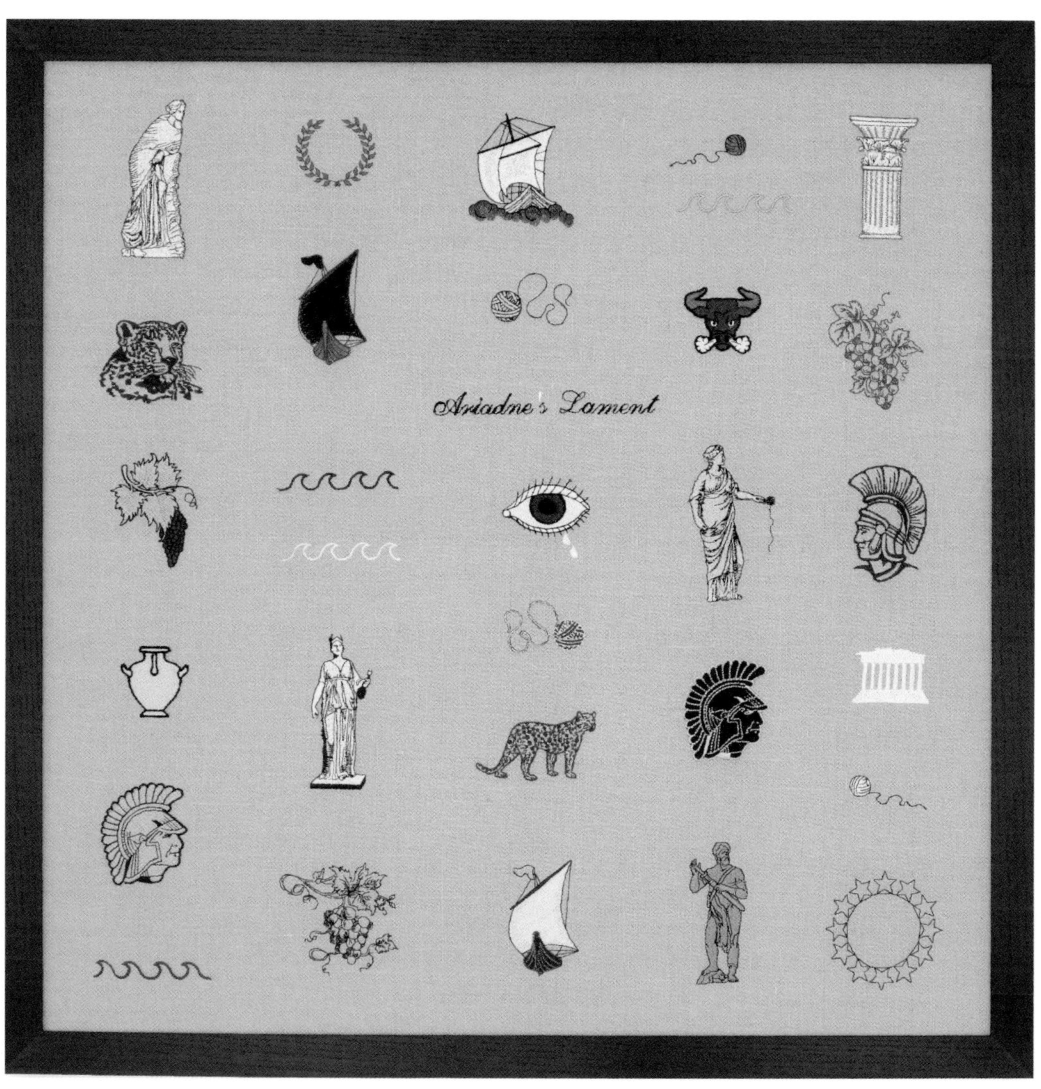

bring out the images' inherent abstract qualities, but also to demonstrate the extent to which the images are constructed and iconic, rather than objective records of reality. She accompanied the photographs with hand-knitted replicas of their central features.

The series "Tierra del Fuegians" (1986–7) derived from early twentieth-century ethnographic photographs of an indigenous people of South America. Elaine juxtaposed the photographs with knitted reproductions of Fuegian body paint that she had also repainted in the photographs. These were the first of her works I saw, and they are an astounding group of images that have stayed in my mind ever since. The conversation between the knitted body and the altered photo body is clear yet thick with nuance and mystery. They evoke the conventions of anthropological displays in natural history museums, while also functioning as abstract art. By repainting the body paint on the photograph, Elaine allows the viewer to really see and appreciate the pattern that was originally painted on another human being's skin. Elaine describes her strategy in these works as "purposefully misreading the patterns as abstraction, which is a Western idea, in order to address the way that seeing is culturally influenced." The knitted Fuegian body that hangs next to the photograph is an eerie double, recognizably human in form yet palpably different.

On the wall of Elaine's bedroom is a full-scale mockup inkjet print of a magnificent tapestry appropriated from Titian's *Bacchus and Adriane*. With a woven blue border and a woven frame, the work also includes a fragment from T.S. Eliot's poem "Sweeney Erect." Elaine's name appears on the work alongside those of Titian and Eliot; she describes these names as "the equivalent of a monogram, a convention from embroidery samplers." The Titian depicts an important moment in the story of Ariadne when she and Bacchus perceive each other for the first time and lock eyes. Between the figures is a large space of blue sky, so beautiful in both the original painting and the print mockup that my eyes lock onto it as well.

Elaine's series "Ariadne's Thread" (2008–2012) addresses the mythological tale of Ariadne, who helped Theseus defeat the Minotaur by giving him a thread to use to find his way into and back out of the Minotaur's labyrinth, only to be abandoned by Theseus afterward. Ariadne is vindicated, however, as she marries the god Bacchus. Elaine has retold the

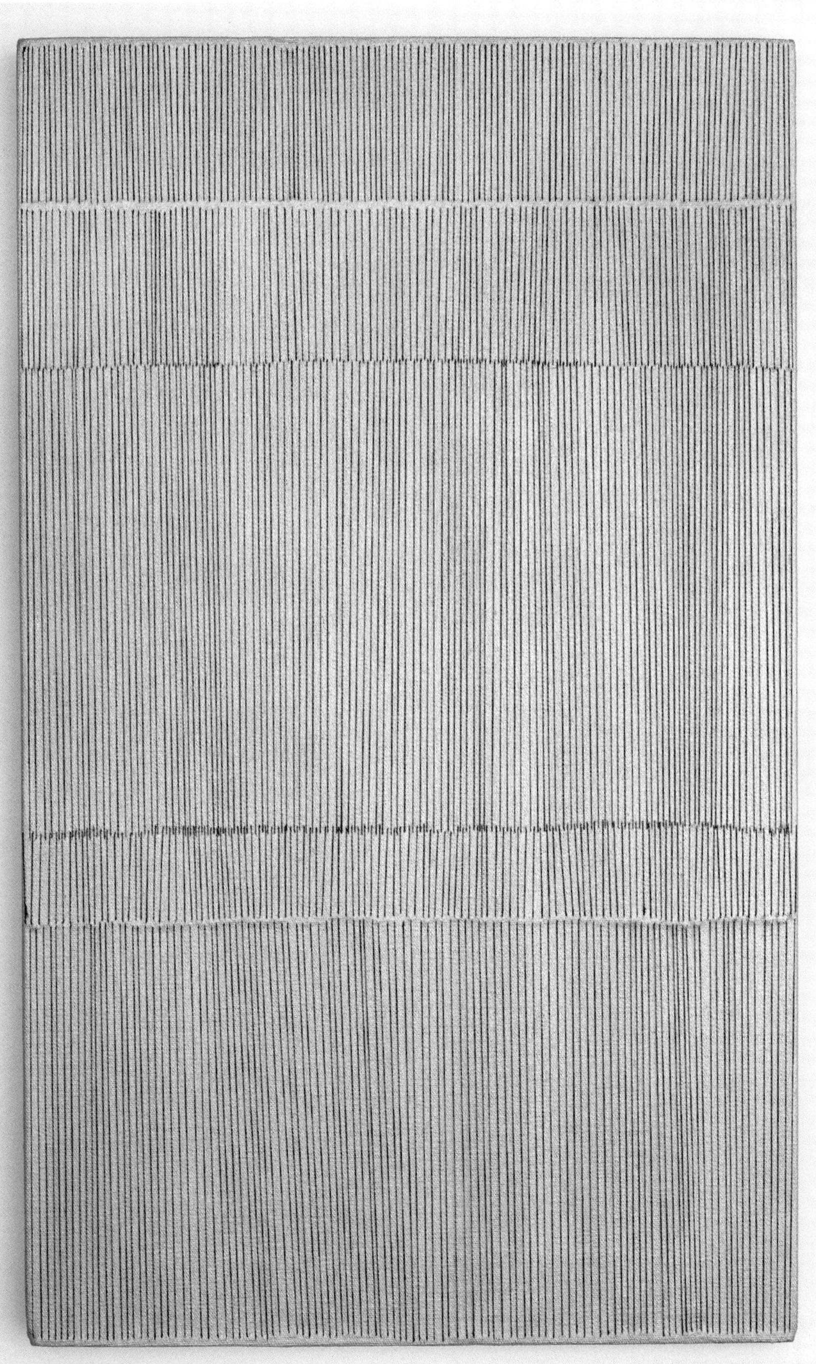

story in a series of seventeen works: sixteen hand-sewn or digitally produced embroideries and one large tapestry made to her specifications in
Belgium. Each work appropriates representations of important moments
in Ariadne's story as rendered by art-historical figures ranging from George
Frederic Watts to Matisse to John Currin. The tapestry, *Paint Me a Cav-
ernous Waste Shore* (2009–10), based on Titian's *Bacchus and Ariadne*
(1520–23), is the capstone of the series. It was included in the 2012
Whitney Biennial. Each embroidery includes a literary quotation from one
of the versions of the story or from a poet or writer who refers to Ariadne
in another context, such as the quotation from T.S. Eliot that serves as the
tapestry's title.

Elaine describes this series as a "minicompendium of the possibilities
of thread," and this is true in both its literal and figurative senses. In ad-
dition to juxtaposing her uses of thread with painting, drawing, and writing, Elaine also juxtaposes mechanical means of production and
reproduction with handicraft and digital technology. The series is an extended meditation on how Ariadne has been depicted in the histories of
art, literature, and even music (since she includes *Ariadne auf Naxos*, the
1912 opera by Strauss and von Hofmannsthal) and the symbolic valences
of the thread and the labyrinth. The work is thus an art-historical survey
that contrasts the linear with the painterly (both translated into embroidery,
of course) and the carefully composed with the spontaneous. Through the
images and quotations Elaine presents, thread becomes the strand of a
narrative; the line of an artist's drawing; or the trace of a handwritten text.
The labyrinth can be a puzzle the world presents us to solve, or it can be
the labyrinth of the inner world we each create for ourselves, as André
Gide suggests in one of the quotations Elaine cites. At the level of narrative, we may identify with the Minotaur, as did Picasso, or with Ariadne,
as does Elaine. The series shows how the mythological tale has become
a matrix for centuries of accreted imagery and ideas. Ariadne-like, Elaine
has always offered us threads with which we can navigate the labyrinths
of reproduction, representation, and reworking that constitute our history
and culture.

As I speak to Elaine one morning, I feel her smiling on the phone. She is glad to talk about her work and her career as an artist. She has worked patiently, worried only about the work and not the career. I ask about her recent success; she has been included in two major exhibitions. One is the Whitney Biennial to which she has been invited for the first time.

The Whitney Annual began in 1934; it became the Whitney Biennial in 1973. Most of the work is by young American artists, though recent biennials have also included international artists. Elaine had four embroideries and the large tapestry in the exhibition. I know she has spoken about this work to school groups at the Whitney, and I asked her what she talked about. Elaine said that people love storytelling, and she told her version of the story of Adriane and the Minotaur. It is a great tale that, in Elaine's telling, is itself like a labyrinth that winds its way around the listener.

The other major exhibition is international, the São Paulo Biennial. This exhibition began in 1951, and this is Elaine's first time showing in it as well, among 110 artists from around the globe. When I heard that Elaine was chosen to be in these shows, I thought, finally this artist who has been working for fifty years is receiving the recognition and acknowledgement she deserves.

Initially, I thought of Elaine primarily as a conceptual artist and her work as particularly smart and witty. But researching her early work, I see her roots in several exquisite works on canvas from the early 1970s, all untitled and all twenty-four by fourteen inches in size. Each one looks like a minimalist pencil drawing on stretched canvas, but in fact each is made of simple and elegant lines of thread that pierce the surface of the canvas. The third one of the set is darker than the first two because of a greater density of sewn lines. Their beauty and elegance are inextricably intertwined, but they are also very funny. They represent a new way of working (especially in the early 1970s) while also participating in traditional conversations about painting and drawing. These hand-sewn marks propose new ideas about what marks are and how they can be made, and about the relationship between how a mark looks on a canvas and what it actually is.

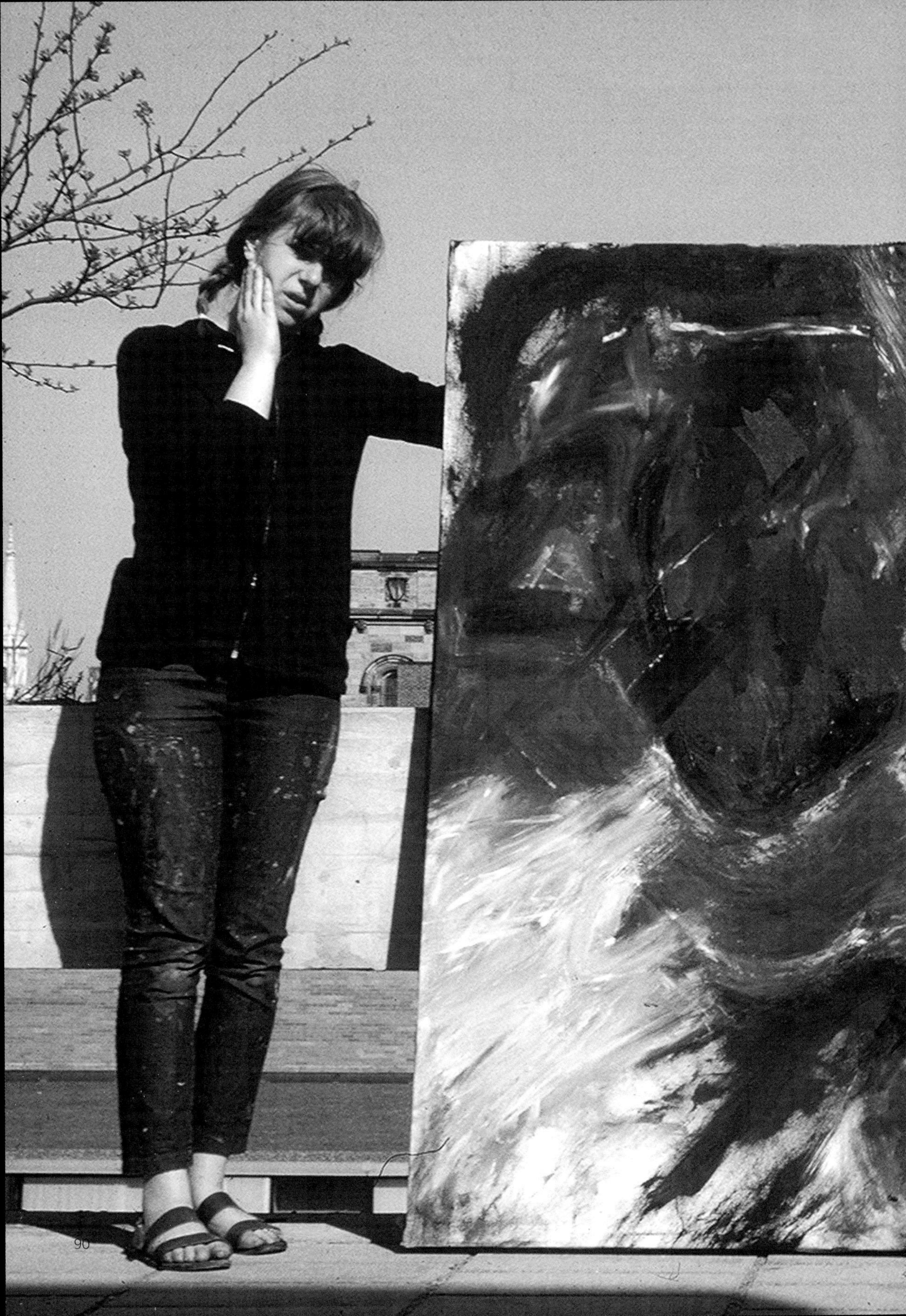

To see where an artist made a first leap in an entirely new direction—one that she has pursued and developed for almost forty years—is like uncovering a secret that the artist is only too happy to reveal. As I look at these works, I smile at the way they prompt me to see the drawn line as a sewn line, as opposed to seeing the sewn line as a drawn line. In art, we usually take drawing to be primary; sewing would necessarily be considered a secondary reference. But Elaine challenges these meanings and priorities by implying the reverse. Thread is as old as paint, after all—perhaps older. Thinking this way, I know that I am under the spell Elaine has woven, and it is indeed a delightful place to be.

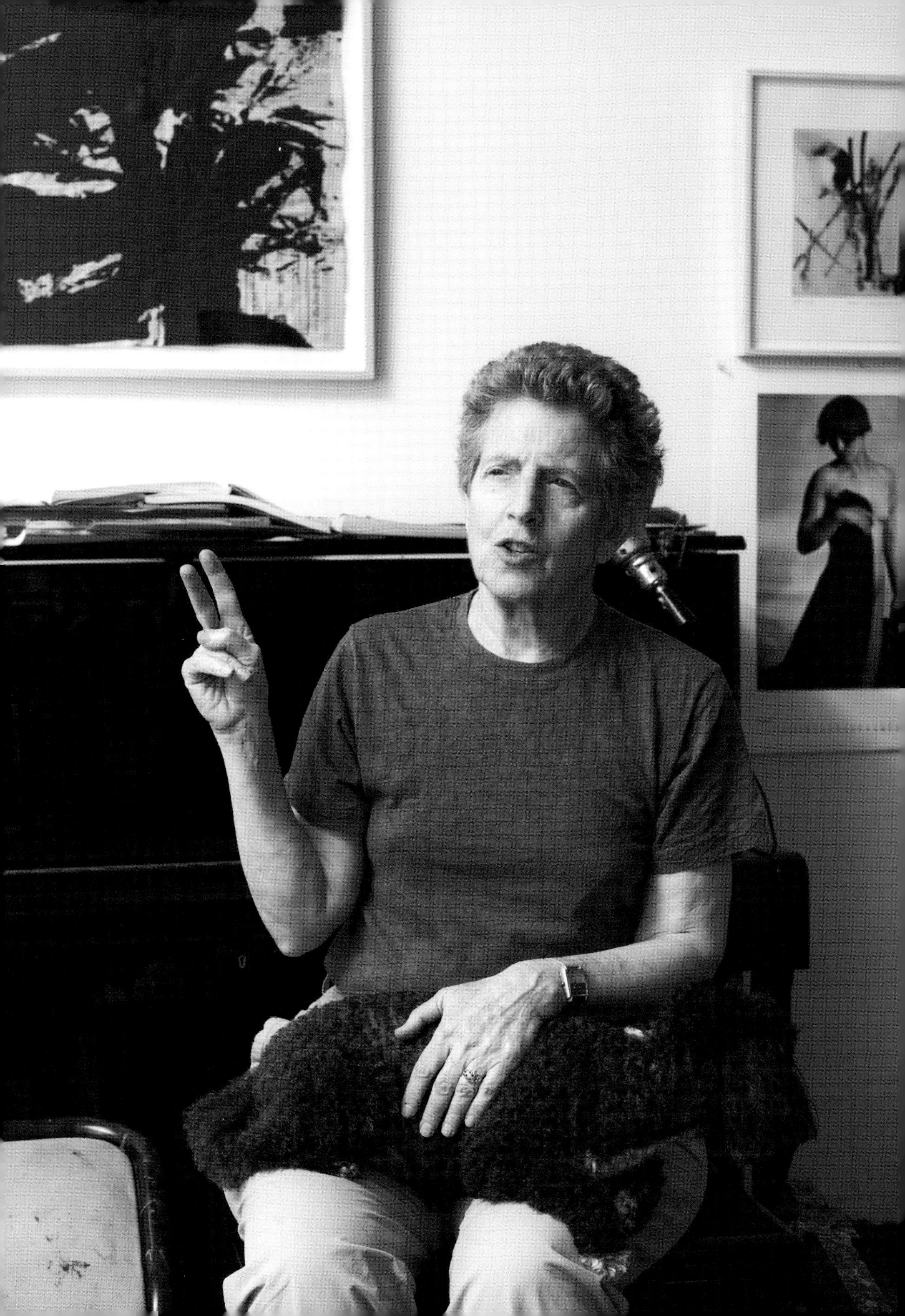

Louise Fishman
Taking the Ball and Running

I

Louise Fishman graciously invited me to her Chelsea studio to talk about her life as an artist. There are no finished works in her studio; Louise has sent off her most recent work to be shown in a solo exhibition at the Paule Anglim Gallery in San Francisco. On the studio walls, though, are several paintings and drawings just begun. As these are works in progress, they do not have the depth and fissures found in Louise's finished paintings and drawings. I find it fascinating to get a glimpse of the structure beneath the skin of the painting. Seeing the skeleton that defines the form, I can't help but anticipate the many layers of paint that will constitute the finished work.

Louise's personal history informs her painting. She loved to play basketball in high school and is still an athletic woman. The physicality of her paintings testifies to this; one can imagine the edges of the canvas as the boundaries and free-throw lines of a basketball court. It is as if Louise passes the ball to herself, takes it and runs to the other side of the court to make another pass, and then jumps and shoots: all through her brush work, paint, and color. You sense the athleticism of her work in the curves and dribbles of paint and the physical rhythm mapped out in her brush-strokes. *All Night and All Day*, a painting from 2008 in oil on canvas, is human sized (sixty-six inches tall by fifty-seven inches wide). The artist can reach from top to bottom; it is a world where she is in control, not only of the paint and the structure but also of the scale. She can move her loaded brush with finesse across or down or around the space she has created. Like any good athlete, performer, or artist, she makes the whole thing look effortless, as if making the mark is simply a natural act.

Louise's work is also deeply informed by her engagement with feminism. As she puts it, "Feminism, the women's movement, the lesbian movement, had a major effect on my work—and my life, of course. It radicalized me, and my work. Gave me a sense of the uniqueness of my position as a woman, as a lesbian, and as an artist. And lots of power!"

The studio is her very private place. Sammy, a small poodle, sleeps or watches as Louise works. This companion is a great witness to her working methods. He is fidelity itself, watching and knowing. Sammy is like a small shadow that is the artist's other self, a sensitive alter ego. Our pets are our other selves, and I so understand that a canine friend is important to an artist's well-being. Louise takes Sammy everywhere—to the studio and on her travels. I am jealous. I would like to take my two dogs with me everywhere, but they are a bit larger and noisier than Sammy.

Louise's finished paintings are built up in many layers to create depth of field. The 2010 paintings that have been shipped to California are mainly vertical compositions. The colors in these 2010 works have a freshness of hue; they radiate light that opens up the space of the paintings. Grays and whites are interspersed with deep dark ultramarines and stratified with small amounts of red and ochre. A wonderfully warm and brightly saturated mixture of pthalo blue and pthalo green meanders around the painted surfaces. The paint is slathered on, thick and luminous, with many fractals of color in every passage. Each rectangle presses up against the next, sometimes overlapping but sometimes breaking like waves on the shore, strong and lively with lavish bravado. Louise's titles, such as *Zero At the Bone* (2010), are provocative yet nevertheless suggest emotion.

Louise's paintings were not always so full of color and air. In her early works, a cornucopia of grays were embedded in a grid that gave the paintings their structure and presence. Describing her use of the grid as a compositional structure, she has said, "The grid comes and goes. It's there now in some ways, but not as obvious. The stricter grid continues to appear from time to time." With *Saga,* a painting from 2010, Louise both returns to and reinvents the grid; the layered paint pulls the structure apart slightly to make it something more.

The child of an artist mother and a father who was the son of a Talmudic scholar (Louise is named for her grandfather), she grew up listening to the radio and reading about the atrocities of the Holocaust. In 1988,

Louise Fishman
Crossing the Rubicon, 2012
Oil on linen
66 x 57 inches
© Louise Fishman
Courtesy Cheim & Read Gallery, New York

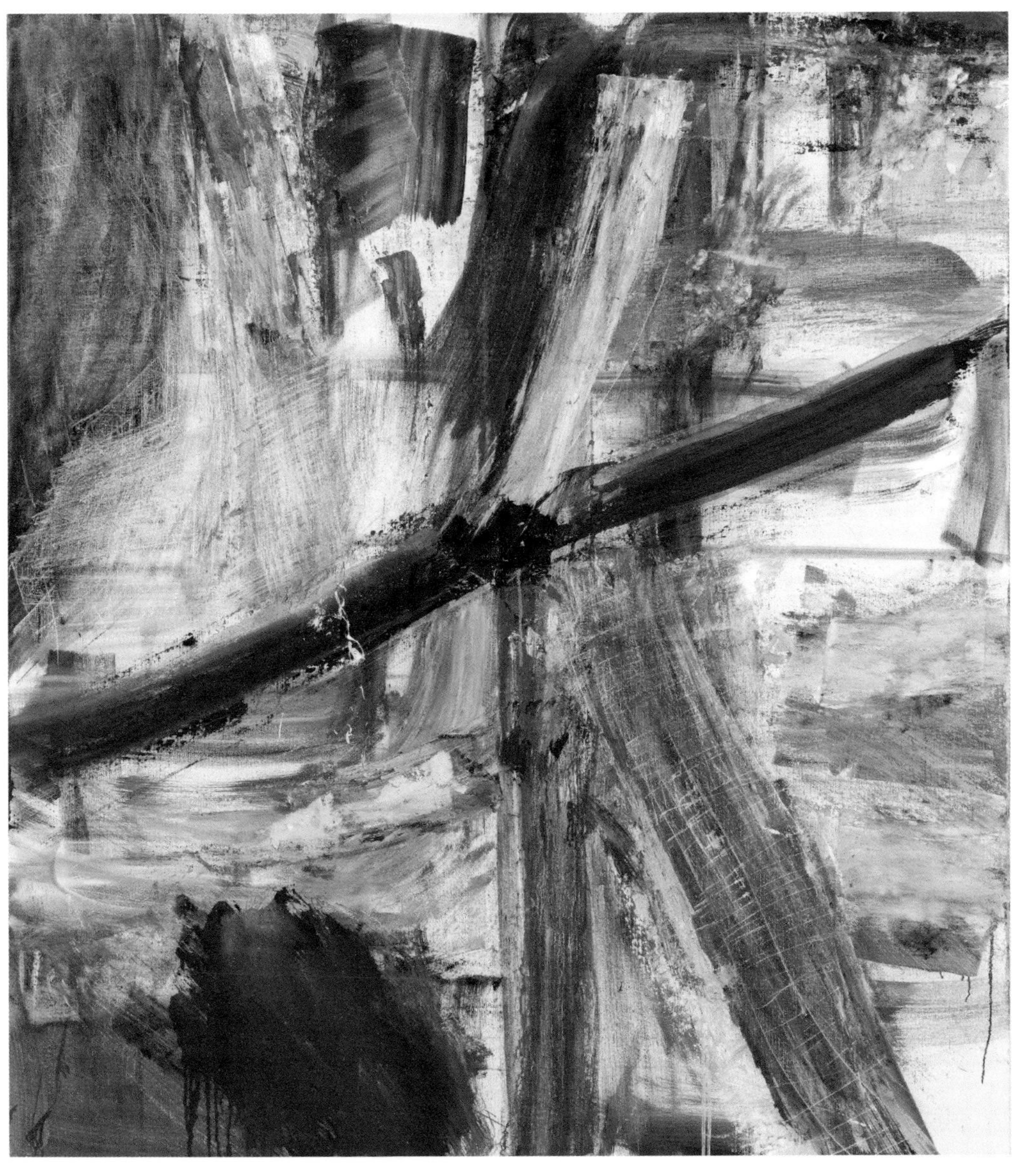

she and a friend, Valerie Furth, a Holocaust survivor, traveled to concentration camps in Czechoslovakia and Poland. The experience provoked feelings of terrible grief. As Louise left Auschwitz, she encountered a pond where the victims' ashes had settled. She impulsively scooped up a handful of the sludge, feeling that she must bring back whatever she could, to preserve Jews in any form possible. She brought the ashes back to her studio, mixed them with beeswax and then paint. Using the ashes in this way turned the paintings into memorials and provided the artist with the catharsis she needed to keep working after the emotionally difficult task of traveling to the sites of the Holocaust.

How does one continue in the studio after feeling such pain and grief? Louise meditates as a way of helping her to "slow down and notice things in the painting process that need to change or deepen." Finally, what is remarkable about her paintings is that you must slow down to really see them. They are about painting—painting that makes you feel the presence of the artist and her life.

II

And life changes. Louise and I have met a few times in the last two years. She has a great bit of news: she is having a romance. I am so delighted. Louise seems light and so happy. The romance is with Ingrid Nyeboe, a friend who was married to another friend, the writer and critic Jill Johnston (1929–2010). I meet Ingrid and Louise in Miami after their prenuptial honeymoon in Venice, where Louise had a residency at the Emily Harvey Foundation. We talked a lot about Venice before she went, a place I adore for its water, the color of the buildings, the way the sky looks over the water, and its people. And, of course, the art.

Sammy was going on this trip as well. I imagined him on the *vaporetto*, his little nose lifted to catch a breeze and savor the scents around him. But I digress. Louise found Venice a visionary delight. Her experience was different from mine, of course, so I am even more interested in what she saw and experienced and what her time there was like. The canals, the

Louise Fishman
Angry Louise, 1973
Acrylic on paper
26 x 40 inches
© Louise Fishman
Courtesy Cheim & Read Gallery, New York

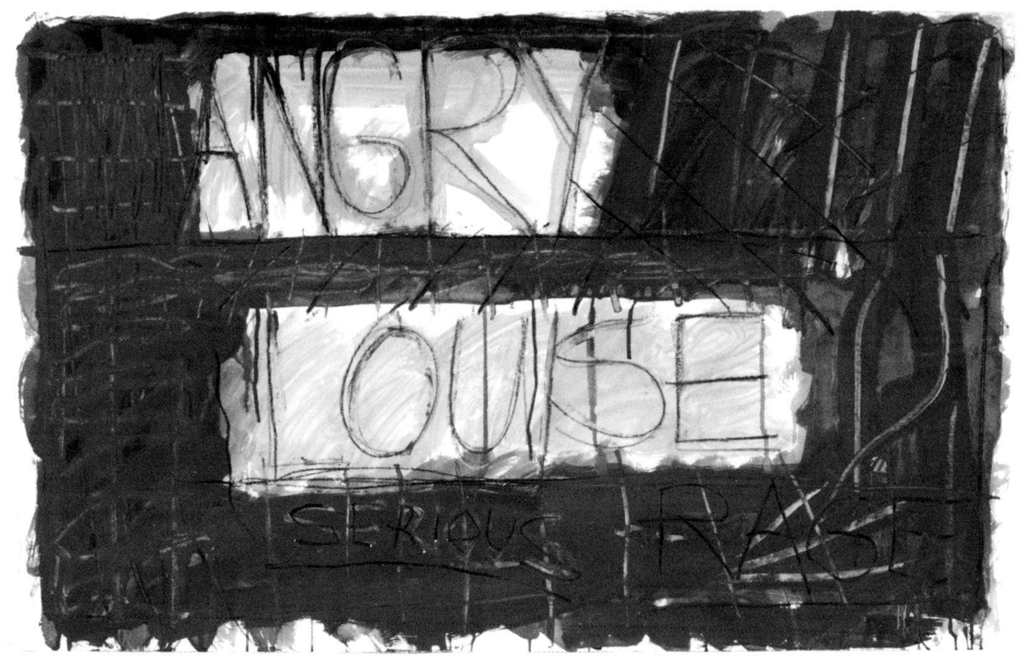

water, the labyrinths of streets all turned out to be the perfect setting for realizing a new body of work that was starting to emerge even before she went on her trip.

When I met Louise with Ingrid while I was in Miami for a quick visit to Art Basel, the big annual art fair, I saw and felt their happiness immediately. Then I saw Louise's post-Venice painting and I knew how good the trip had been. It made me happy to see that Louise had clearly understood Venice, as not everyone gets that place so overloaded with tourists, pigeons, and smells that are not particularly pretty. Louise told me the Titians were an incredible inspiration during her time there, and I imagined her sitting in the Scuola Grande di San Rocco immersed in viewing the large works. I know the street they stayed on; it has the best coffee shop one can imagine. If you know painters, you know that most of us need, not just want, caffeine. I could almost hear the Venetian dialect floating through the *calli* and my favorite restaurants and squares.

In Miami, I also saw a series of monoprints that Louise made with her printer, Sue Oehme, in Steamboat Springs, Colorado. The monoprints are small and presented in portfolio sets, small objects to be taken out and shared and then put back away, like jewels or rare spices. Ingrid tells me Louise has been working well; she made watercolors in Venice that seemed to just flow out of her, so perfect was the place and time.

I remember how I first learned about Louise's work. A male colleague had just come back from the MacDowell Colony and told me about some women artists he had met there. When I came upon a series of Louise's small, thickly painted works from 1980 in a gallery, I realized she was one of the artists he mentioned. I immediately fell for these works. The impasto of paint was sometimes scraped off and the compositions swirled. I recently told Louise that this was how I came to know her work, and she remembered my friend, since there were not many painters at MacDowell at the time. I laughed as she told me of the French easel that he used when he went off into the woods and fields to paint.

But it is her show of recent work at her gallery Cheim & Read, in the fall of 2012, and its companion show of fifty years of Louise's work at the Tilton Gallery, that allow me to understand her work better. There is a wonderful untitled cloth work from 1971, which functions like a gray tonal grid painting except that the physicality of the cloth changes the work by making the composition more pronounced. I wonder about this work, what its references are, what Louise was pursuing in her work when she made this. It looks like something you might use on a boat with a brown cord and some kind of sign for stormy weather. It is a beautiful grid that functions as a structure, though the emphasis on the object's physical qualities pushes it toward abstraction.

In the show at Tilton, although there is great variation of periods and themes, the tonality, even in the large paintings, is darker and grayer than in her most recent work. It included a selection from *Angry Women* (1973), a wonderful suite of drawings in which Louise uses text to expel her anger on behalf of herself, her female heroes, relatives, friends, and lovers. The marks and writing in these drawings are so powerful, the gestures of the marks so angry that I hope the artist found the making of these as cathartic as I did looking at them. The paintings at the Tilton show are large and wonderful, expressive and rhythmic. Louise employs a palette of blacks and grays, using thick paint that has been scraped, rolled on, or painted with large brushes to impart a feeling of power to the work.

The new work at Cheim & Read is post-Venice and shows Louise engaging with color. They are not like the little paintings made at the MacDowell Colony but are light and bright in both color and stroke. Yet these paintings move. *Crossing the Rubicon* (2012) is an asterisk-like composition in which brushstrokes cross and meet in the middle. I love that Louise has titled this work with the idea that you cannot go back.

Louise also had a museum show in 2012–2013, perhaps her most important. Called "Generations," it was at the Woodmere Art Museum in Philadelphia, and it included Louise, her mother, Gertrude Fisher-Fishman, who is still alive at ninety-seven and only stopped painting four years ago, and her aunt, Razel Kapustin, who died in 1968 at the age of sixty. Louise was instrumental in putting together this exhibition. She really wanted to look at her roots as an artist, her Aunt Razel being particularly dear to her and important as a painter. Louise and I spoke a few days after she had given an emotional lecture at the museum about the connections and shared inspirations between these three painters, family members, and women. Chaim Soutine, who used paint like a lush, physical substance

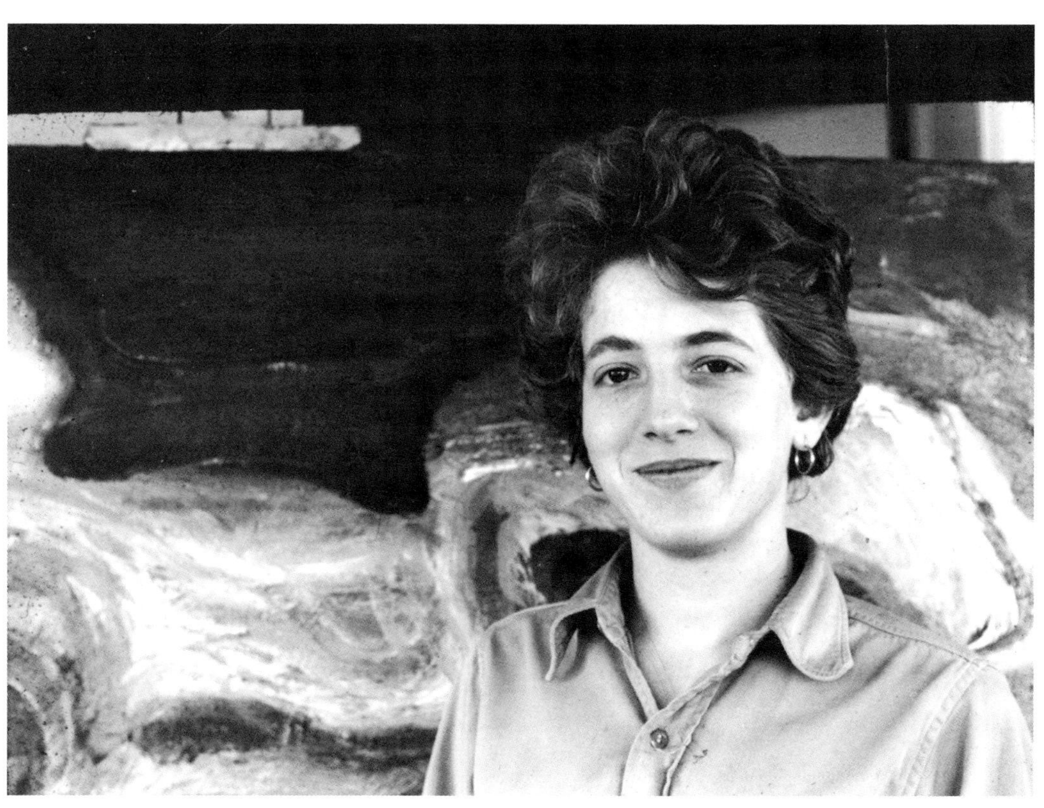

that wrapped around the representational parts of his paintings, was a great influence on all three, as was the emotive brushwork of Abstract Expressionism. But even if such influences are visible, each woman has her own distinct voice.

I believe Louise still converses about painting with her mother in a dialogue that began many decades ago, and the show is a testament to the love they feel for each other. Louise tells me she is thankful for the life she was given as an artist. It is a life of freedom, of ideas, thoughts, passion, and creativity. She communicates this understanding of the life of the artist through her paintings, and she is glad to have us listen.

Deanna Sirlin in
her studio, 2013
Photo: Madison
Michelle

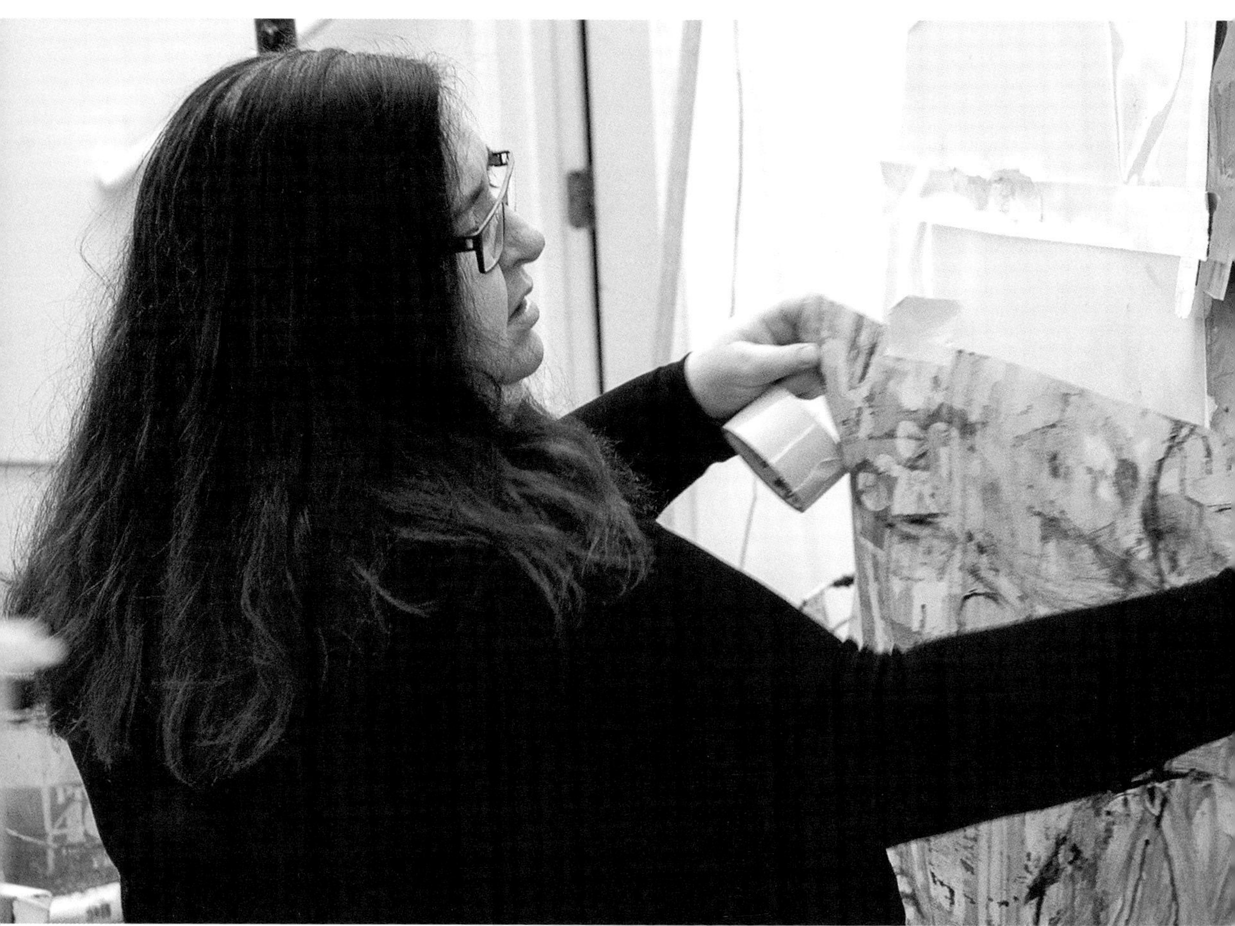

After

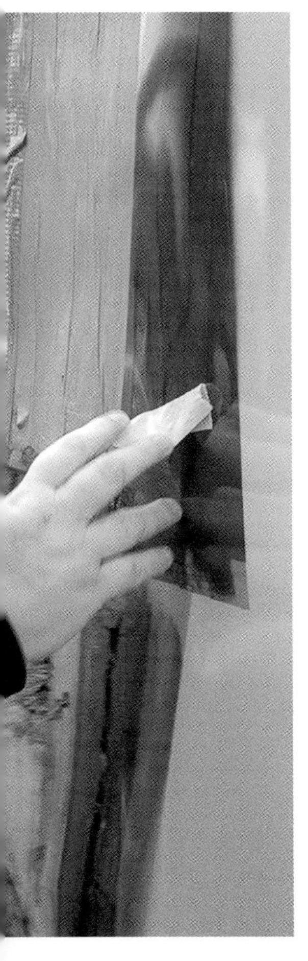

I have visited these significant woman artists and maintained contact in person or by phone. I have gone to see their shows, read their reviews, and pondered catalogue essays. Since starting this pilgrimage I feel more thankful to these artists than ever. As an artist, I have discovered some part of myself in each of them. Surprisingly, it is not always the part I expected.

Although some of these artists do not know one another, there are still significant connections among them. Some go back decades, some go back to the feminist movement, and some were in the same galleries or the same groups. Now they all seem to be on their own, floating through the art world and finally rising to the top, having major exhibitions, experimenting with new technologies, and being included in important biennials, retrospectives, and shows that analyze their early work in relationship to what they are currently all about.

Many of these women came of age as artists around the same time, which may explain why many of them have made significant use of the grid, a 1970s phenomenon, in their work. Joyce Kozloff's early compositions are hung on the grid: elegant, geometrically patterned abstractions that morphed into her Pattern and Decoration work, with sources that spanned the globe. Louise Fishman actually wove the drawing itself into her grid; she punched holes in gray-stained canvas and sewed the pieces into a grid using a kind of raw twine. Elaine Reichek is still enamored of the grid as the support for her sewing, knitting, and crocheting, much of which is digital—the ultimate grid. Pat Steir and Joan Snyder laid and analyzed their brushstrokes upon the grid. Even Ursula von Rydingsvard used a grid method of sorts: strips of commercially milled cedar beams are all cut in cubic lengths of four by four inches by the length she needs to make her sculpture. Although the use of the grid ties these artists together, it is where and how they have departed from it that I find most interesting.

Their processes have changed over the years, and my perception of the work has changed as I have changed and matured as an artist. My revisiting their art is crucial. Some circumstances have changed; now there are many female art professors teaching in universities, and young women artists have almost the same advantages as young male artists, but not totally. There is still a leap to be made in terms of how many woman artists make it into museums and private collections, have full-time art dealers, and are written about critically in books as well as magazines.

Of course I could have written this book with a mixture of male and female artists. When I first started looking at contemporary art, almost all of it was made by men in the galleries I visited. I cannot think of more than a few Pop artists who are female, or 1980s expressionists who were not male. The history of art is the history of art made by men, and it was the women who had to make a path and create a new language to articulate their ideas.

So after thirty years of looking I decided I needed more information; I needed to know what set these artists apart. The connection of both the body and the personality to the work, and the process of making it, are now much clearer to me.

But most important, I see that over the course of making artwork for thirty to fifty or more years, the work has a need and a presence all its own. The artist just needs the time, physical strength, and financial support to realize the many works that are inside of her. After periods of not being able to work, or not wanting to work, years of thinking or not thinking but allowing the work to flow and just be released from the artist, that is the time when the work has the most clarity and power. This is when the artist gathers and uses every bit of knowledge and ability and thought and emotion to realize the work.

Deanna Sirlin
Map, 2012
10 x 5.5 inches
Mixed media
© Deanna Sirlin
Courtesy of the artist

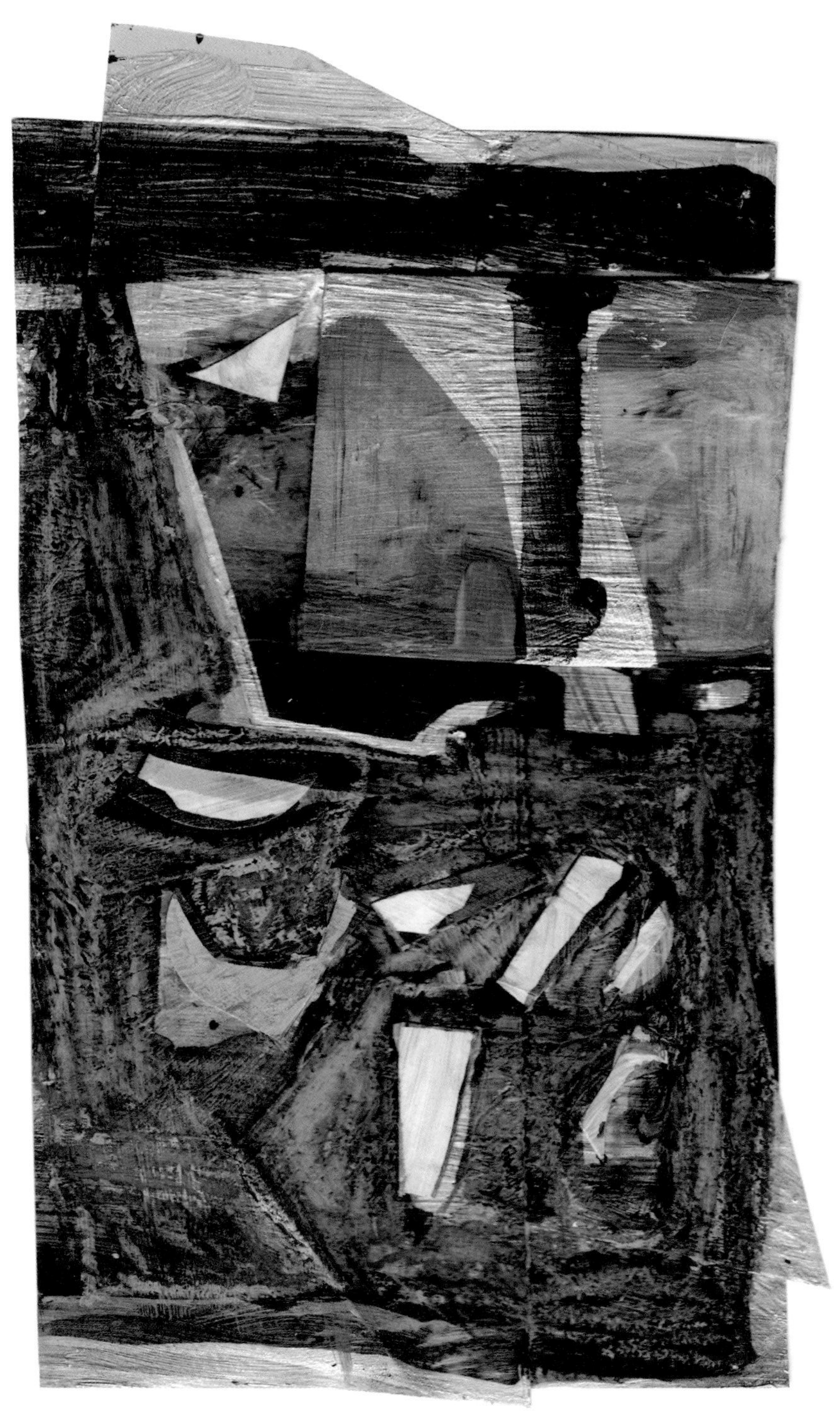

List of Illustrations

Cover
Deanna Sirlin
Map, 2012 (detail)
Mixed media
10 x 5.5 inches
© Deanna Sirlin
Courtesy of the artist

Where It Begins
Deanna Sirlin
Progress, 2013
Mixed media
60 x 80 inches
© Deanna Sirlin

Deanna Sirlin in her studio, 2013
Photo: Madison Michelle

Betty Woodman
Born in Norwalk, Connecticut, 1930

Portrait of Betty Woodman, circa 2009

Betty Woodman
Peruvian Vase and Shadow, 1984
Glazed earthenware, epoxy resin, lacquer, paint
23 x 28 x 15 inches
© Betty Woodman
Courtesy Salon 94, New York

Betty Woodman
Installation view in the Cane Acres Plantation House
Dining Room
Playing House, Brooklyn Museum
February 24–August 26, 2012
Photo: Hiroki Kobayashi
© Betty Woodman
Courtesy Salon 94, New York

Betty Woodman
On the Way to Mexico, 2012

Glazed earthenware, epoxy resin, lacquer, acrylic paint
34 x 35 x 9 inches
Photo: Eli Ping Weinberg
© Betty Woodman
Courtesy Salon 94, New York

Portrait of Betty Woodman, circa 1996
Photo: George Woodman

Ursula von Rydingsvard
Born in Deensen, Germany, 1942

Portrait of Ursula von Rydingsvard with *Conjugation*,
2012
Photo: Andria Morales
© Ursula von Rydingsvard
Courtesy Galerie Lelong, New York

Ursula von Rydingsvard
Luba, 2010
Cedar, graphite, bronze
212 x 117 x 88 inches
Photo: Jerry L. Thompson
© Ursula von Rydingsvard
Courtesy Galerie Lelong, New York

Ursula von Rydingsvard
Damski Czepek, 2006
Polyurethane resin
132 x 406 x 364 inches
Photo: Etienne Frossard
© Ursula von Rydingsvard
Courtesy Galerie Lelong, New York

Ursula von Rydingsvard at Battery Park City landfill,
New York, with *St. Martin's Dream*, 1980
Photo: David Allison
© Ursula von Rydingsvard
Courtesy Galerie Lelong, New York

Joyce Kozloff
Born in Somerville, New Jersey, 1942

Joyce Kozloff in front of *JEEZ*, 2011 (in progress)
Photo: Morgan Rachel Levy

Joyce Kozloff
L'Afrique, 2012
Acrylic, collage, and archival inkjet print
35.75 x 31.25 inches
Photo: Kevin Noble
© Joyce Kozloff
Courtesy DC Moore Gallery, New York

Joyce Kozloff
Cincinnati Fireplace, 1980
Glazed tiles, board
60 x 114.5 inches
Photo: Ron Forth
© Joyce Kozloff
Courtesy DC Moore Gallery, New York

Joyce Kozloff, 1980
Photo: Max Kozloff

Jane Freilicher
Born in Brooklyn, New York, 1924

Jane Freilicher, 1984
Photo: Nancy Crampton

Jane Freilicher
Study in Blue and Gray, 2011
Oil on linen
24 x 24 inches
Photo: Alan Wiener
© Jane Freilicher
Courtesy Tibor de Nagy Gallery, New York

Jane Freilicher
Afternoon in October, 1976
Oil on linen
51 x 77 inches
© Jane Freilicher
Courtesy Tibor de Nagy Gallery, New York

Fairfield Porter at work on portrait of Jane Freilicher
and her daughter
Jane and Elizabeth, 1967
Photo courtesy Fairfield Porter Archives
Parrish Art Museum, Water Mill, New York

Jennifer Bartlett
Born in Long Beach, California, 1941

Jennifer Bartlett, 2011
Photo: Nancy Brooks Brody

Jennifer Bartlett
In the Garden Drawing #33, 1980
Pen and ink on paper
9.5 x 26 inches
© Jennifer Bartlett

Jennifer Bartlett
Amagansett Diptych #2, 2007
Oil on canvas
96 x 192 inches
© Jennifer Bartlett

Jennifer Bartlett, 1975
South Hampton, New York

Pat Steir
Born in Newark, New Jersey, in 1940

Pat Steir, 2012
Photo: Rebecca Robertson

Pat Steir
White Splash on Black, Black Splash on White, 2009
Oil on canvas
84 x 84 inches
© Pat Steir
Courtesy Cheim & Read Gallery, New York

Pat Steir
Twenty-One Musicians on a White Elephant, 1991
Oil on canvas
173 x 115 inches
© Pat Steir
Courtesy Cheim & Read Gallery, New York

Pat Steir, 2008
Photo: William Steen

Joan Snyder
Born in Highland Park, New Jersey, 1940

Portrait of Joan Snyder, 2007
Photo: Marni Majorelle

Joan Snyder
Symphony IV, 1977
Oil, fabric, paper, glitter on canvas
60 x 120 inches
© Joan Snyder

Joan Snyder
Still, 2011
Oil, acrylic, papier-mâché, twigs, glass beads,
cheesecloth, silk, burlap, rosebuds on linen
48 x 63 inches
© Joan Snyder
Courtesy of the artist

Portrait of Joan in the 1970s
Photo: Larry Fink

Elaine Reichek
Born in New York, New York, 1943

Elaine Reichek in front of *Swatches: B&W 1–25*, 2007
Photo: Paul Kennedy
© Elaine Reichek
Courtesy of Nicole Klagsbrun Gallery, New York
and Shoshana Wayne Gallery, Santa Monica

Elaine Reichek
Ariadne's Lament, 2009
Digital embroidery on linen
27.5 x 26.5 inches
Photo: Paul Kennedy
© Elaine Reichek
Collection of the Museum of Fine Arts, Boston

Elaine Reichek
Untitled #21, 1973
Gesso, acrylic, thread, and graphite on canvas
24 x 14 inches
Photo: Paul Kennedy
© Elaine Reichek
Courtesy of the artist

Elaine Reichek, 1964
Paul Rudolph Building, Yale University, New Haven,
Connecticut
(photographer unknown)

Louise Fishman
Born in Philadelphia, Pennsylvania, 1939

Louise Fishman, 2012
Photo: Brian Buckley

Louise Fishman
Crossing the Rubicon, 2012
Oil on linen
66 x 57 inches
© Louise Fishman
Courtesy Cheim & Read Gallery, New York

Louise Fishman
Angry Louise, 1973
Acrylic on paper
26 x 40 inches
© Louise Fishman
Courtesy Cheim & Read Gallery, New York

Louise Fishman in the studio, circa 1980

After
Deanna Sirlin in her studio, 2013
Photo: Madison Michelle

Deanna Sirlin
Map, 2012
10 x 5.5 inches
Mixed media
© Deanna Sirlin
Courtesy of the artist

About the Author
Deanna Sirlin, 2013
Photo: Evie Saleh

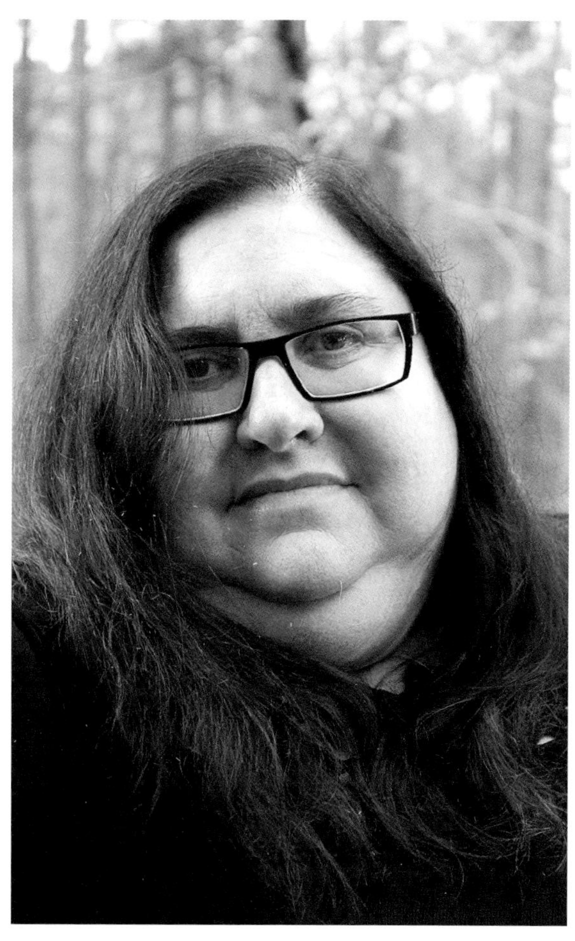

Deanna Sirlin,
2013
Photo: Evie Saleh

About the Author

Deanna Sirlin is an American painter and artist born in Brooklyn, New York, whose studio is at her farm outside of Atlanta, Georgia. She has exhibited her work both locally and internationally at numerous venues including the New Orleans Museum of Art, Louisiana; the Shenzhen Institute, China; and Kunsthaus Nürnberg, Germany. Her solo exhibitions include the High Museum of Art, Atlanta; the Antayla Cultural Center, Turkey; the Centre for Recent Drawing, London, UK; and Ca' Foscari University of Venice, Italy. She recently had a solo exhibition at M55 Art in New York City as an invited guest of the gallery.

Sirlin is editor-in-chief of *The Art Section: An Online Journal of Art and Cultural Commentary*. She has written reviews for the magazines *Art Papers* and *Creative Loafing* in Atlanta. Sirlin was selected to participate in the art writers' mentoring program sponsored by Creative Capital and the Warhol Foundation. Through this program she was mentored by author Hayden Herrera. Sirlin has been a Yaddo fellow and an artist-in-residence for the city of Nürnberg, Germany, and at the Château de Padiès, Lempaut, France. *She's Got What It Takes: Contemporary American Woman Artists in Dialogue* is her first book.

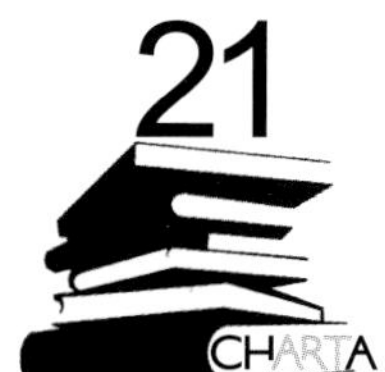 CHARTA

To find out more about Charta,
and to learn about our most recent
publications, visit

www.chartaartbooks.it

Printed in April 2013
by Bianca & Volta, Truccazzano (MI)
for Edizioni Charta